BORN MISSIONARY

The Islay Walden Story

By Margo Lee Williams

Foreword by
Thomas D. Rush
Author of *Reality's Pen* and Walden Family Historian

Published by Margo Lee Williams
Personal Prologue

14612 Edelmar Drive
Silver Spring, MD 20906

Printed in the United States of America

ISBN-13: 9780578810362 (Paperback)
ISBN: 9780578810379 (eBook)
Library of Congress Control Number: 2021904917

Acknowledgements

Few things can be accomplished without the support of others. This book is no exception. Special thanks must go to those who have been especially encouraging, including Harvey Boone, Christine Hill, Ashley Hoover, Marvin Jones, Elbert Lassiter, Thomas Rush, and Victoria Price. Special remembrance is due also for the late Evie Ruth Grady, great grandniece of Islay Walden, who shared family stories so willingly, and for the late Carolyn Neely Hager, historian in the Randolph Room at the Randolph County Regional Library, in Asheboro, North Carolina, who first introduced me to Islay Walden. Special thanks also go to Russell Gasero (retired) and Matthew Gasero, Archivists for the Reformed Church in America, at the New Brunswick Theological Seminary in New Jersey, and L. McKay Whatley, Director of Local History and Genealogy Services, Randolph Room, Randolph County Regional Library. Thanks also go to my early readers whose observations and editorial suggestions greatly improved the manuscript. A big note of gratitude also goes to Abigail Fleming, my editor and Rachael Cox, book designer, who were able to bring a professional polish to my efforts, making this story that much more enjoyable for the reader.

There is also special note of thanks due to Edward Rich and Thomas Rush. Ed Rich is a lifelong resident of the Strieby area, in southwest Randolph County. He is also a local historian and artist who graciously agreed to paint a portrait of Islay Walden for the cover. Thomas Rush is a native of Asheboro, writer, and Walden family researcher. Thomas generously agreed to write the foreword, providing his insights as a Walden descendant.

There is always one more special person to thank, Jerry Laughlin. Jerry grew up in the neighboring community of Lassiter Mill. He is a descendant of those early Strieby Church members who were gathered for worship and education by Islay. Now Jerry lovingly cares for the church and cemetery where Islay Walden, his wife and fellow teacher, Elinora Farmer Walden, and so many other early church members rest in eternal peace.

Dedicated to

All the students and teachers in Washington, D.C.; New Brunswick, New Jersey; and especially Strieby, North Carolina, who were inspired and encouraged by Islay Walden's passion for education, love of humanity, and missionary zeal.

And when he said, Go forth and preach,
Did he not also bid to teach?
Although my talent may be small,
My Saviour will require it all

— From "Introductory Verses," in *Miscellaneous Poems*
Which the Author Dedicates to the Cause of Education and Humanity,
by Islay Walden, 1873

Table of Contents

Table of Illustrations

Foreword

Tuning into my Momma's (Hortense Chrisco Rush) inner being developed a kind of ghostly, mysterious whisper within my soul, a silent story of a profound family heritage that she and her family carried within their DNA. It was both a great potential for future achievement coterminous with a profound family legacy. In my youth, I was scant on the details.

As with many people, it took a shock to my mortal being, the death of my father, Pearl Rush, in 2007, to push me into the family research with which Providence seemed to be cajoling me, creating a research SOS that still calls me. As fate would have it, I was immediately led to Robbins, North Carolina, Momma's family homeplace. It was a location I knew to contain the long-hidden secrets that had been calling to my soul. For whatever reason, I intuited that there was going to be much for me to learn on the Walden side of my mother's family. Thus, it came as no surprise that it was there, in Robbins, that God gave me one of the most profound family gifts that I have ever received in the form of a more-than-a year relationship with Mary Brower Sawyer, a mind-blowingly lucid and sagacious 102-year-old distant cousin, on Momma's Walden side. We spent the last year of Aunt Mary's (as she was called) life getting to know each other and sharing stories.

Aunt Mary was a goldmine of family information, as she recalled the names and details of numerous relatives from another era. She had no problem sharing all that she knew, both in terms of her own life and her knowledge of the wider family. She gave me a great deal of literature as well as VHS tapes to review related to our family. It was during one of our conversations that Aunt Mary took the liberty of introducing me to someone she said was a relative from a forgotten age, a man named Islay Walden.

The introduction began with an explanation that Islay had been a productive writer prior to the end of slavery, writing poetry at that time. It was said that when he was told that he was a poet, he inquired to know what that was. Islay had been writing poetry before he even knew that there was a name for it. Aunt Mary said she had some writings of his, but I never got to review them. She also talked about Islay's skill with numbers and how his owner would use him to do calculations. Nevertheless, it was early in that first conversation about Islay that she made it clear to me that he was a man of both visionary spirituality and intelligence, a man who was way ahead of his time. I knew Aunt Mary well enough to know that by spelling out Islay's legacy, she was tacitly relaying the message that his life holds meaning for all of humankind, not just for the Walden family.

Aunt Mary had planted the seeds of curiosity about Islay's life within my consciousness. There was so much about him that appealed to me, making me yearn to know more of the details of his life. I imagine it was the combination of my destined family research and the curiosity that Islay inspired that brought me eventually into a writing and research friendship with the author of this volume, Margo Williams.

I originally met Margo when I attended a discussion on her first book on her ancestor Miles Lassiter, and through that discussion and reading her book, we both realized that our respective Lassiter/Walden families had a relationship that went back more than one hundred years, with both families planting roots in rural Randolph County. Though her first book on her ancestor Miles Lassiter talked about Islay Walden, her second book, *From Hill Town to Strieby*, went into more detail about him and really laid the groundwork for this current book. I think that it is fair to say that Margo's research for her two previous books helped to fuel her interest in Islay Walden.

Though Islay was nearly blind, he was a visionary genius. In the late 1800s, among his many other accomplishments, Islay managed to publish two volumes of poetry. Since Islay was a pioneering African American poet, those who have chosen to assess him have chosen to do so primarily through a literary lens. Certainly. Islay's literary accomplishments are worthy of attention, but it is Margo's point that to put him exclusively, or even primarily, under a literary spotlight, does him a disservice and misses the mark for what she feels are his two primary callings in life: one, his commitment to God through the ministry, and two, his obsession with the education of his people.

When Margo put the appropriate focus on Islay's ministry and educational efforts, she filled in a piece to the family jigsaw puzzle within my soul, answering some of the secretly whispered questions about Walden family history that, as a child, I did not even know to ask. Her explosion of information is consistent with my intuition that there was some unknown body of knowledge out there about my mother's lineage that was quite simply extraordinary, a legacy trumpeting a message to the larger world. It combined the dogged effort to overcome obstacles with following the mission to love and serve God. This ideal was then married to Islay's relentless quest for education for African Americans. The themes and principles put forth in this Islay Walden narrative are consistent with the ethos of what it meant to grow up within my family home. This biography reminds me of the information that I received from Aunt Mary, another goldmine for our heritage. Sensitive, detailed, and buoyant family histories of this type are like God reaching his hand down from Heaven to deliver a gift. Its tangible reality is its sacredness, and for this alone, the Walden family will be forever indebted to Margo Williams. Thank you! Thank You! Thank you!

—Thomas D. Rush, Walden family historian and author of *Reality's Pen: Reflections on Family, History & Culture*

Introduction

Over the years that I have been researching Islay Walden's life and ministry, I have been struck by how much misinformation there is about him. He was not a Presbyterian minister. He attended New Brunswick Theological Seminary, the seminary of the Dutch Reformed Church, now Reformed Church of America. The Presbyterian seminary in New Jersey is Princeton, but Princeton reportedly turned him down when he requested admission. Similarly, he did not return to Randolph County, North Carolina, after seminary as a Presbyterian minister. Unfortunately, the Reformed Church had no missionary posts available in the South, so he signed with the American Missionary Association, which was closely associated with the Congregational Church. Indeed, it was a Congregational Church that Islay founded upon returning to Randolph County. Perhaps, most significantly, he was not the son of William D. Walden. Islay was likely a relative but not his son. So, who was Islay Walden?

Islay Walden is primarily remembered as a blind, formerly enslaved, late-nineteenth-century African American poet. His work attracted the attention of Arthur A. Schomberg and John Edward Bruce and was included among the works gathered for the first collection of literary classics at what would become the Schomberg Center for Research in Black Culture in New York City. However, when Islay returned to North Carolina in 1879, after twelve years in Washington, D.C., and New Brunswick, New Jersey, he did not do so as a poet, but as a minister and educator.

Poetry served Islay well in the years between leaving North Carolina in 1867 and returning in 1879. It helped him raise money for his studies, but his passion was the education and "up-lift" of the people. In both Washington, D.C., and New Brunswick, New Jersey, he started successful Sabbath school programs for children of color and a mutual aid society for the adults. He brought that same passionate energy back to Randolph County, North Carolina, to create a successful church and school.

Despite Islay's apparent popularity in Washington and New Jersey, there is only limited information about his life. Unfortunately, there has not been any serious, scholarly interest in his life. Most biographical sketches repeat the same few paragraphs, usually taken from the sketches that appeared in the introductions to his two books of poetry. However, his poetry often took a biographical turn, explaining what he was doing, where he was doing it, and with whom.

The poems in his first volume, *Miscellaneous Poems*, are not arranged chronologically, but if one attempts to read them chronologically, one realizes that he is telling the reader about his life, challenges, fears, hopes, and successes, primarily while living in Washington, D.C., as a student at Howard University. While he references time that he spent in New Jersey during the summer, with one exception and that more accurately a letter, he did not write any of the poems in *Miscellaneous Poems* while in New Jersey.

Islay's poetry took a different turn when he went to New Jersey to attend seminary. His second poetry volume was published shortly after arriving in New Brunswick. However, these poems are not expressions of his thoughts and reflections on his life and dreams. These poems, called *Sacred Hymns*, were published for the purpose of raising money for his school expenses. Thus, there was no additional information about his life in his introduction, with few exceptions. On the other hand, his activities as a seminarian at the New Brunswick Theological Seminary attracted continuous attention from the local newspaper, the *Daily Times*. Without the news articles in the *Daily Times*, almost nothing would be known about his life in New Jersey.

Similarly, when he left New Jersey, the extensive news article in the *Goldsboro Messenger* that Islay wrote about his return trip to North Carolina provided some insight into his experiences and attitudes. Articles and reports submitted to the *American Missionary* (which published information on the missions and missionaries of the American Missionary Association) provided information on his life and work after returning to Randolph County. Sadly, it appears he never published any poetry again after leaving New Jersey, nor any other biographical essays or articles after returning to Randolph County. Still, those writings that are available have provided insights into his life and helped to rescue him from obscurity.

Perhaps the most striking discovery was about someone he never mentioned — Frederick Douglass. It is curious that the single most prominent African American in Washington, D.C., who was a trustee of Howard University while Islay was a student there, was never mentioned even once in any of Islay's writings. It is almost certain their paths crossed at some point, yet Islay makes no mention of him — not even a reference to seeing him at a public event. It is difficult to believe there is not a story there. Perhaps one day it will be revealed.

Ordination

Notices had been appearing for months. The time had finally come. It had been a long and difficult journey with many obstacles — the impact of enslavement, near blindness, poverty, illiteracy, life away from family and friends — but he had made it. He had overcome them all. Graduation and ordination were just two days away, but first, he would preach on Sunday at the local African Methodist Episcopal (AME) Church.[1] Mount Zion AME Church was the oldest and most important African American church in New Brunswick, New Jersey. Mount Zion was (and is) not only the oldest African American Church in New Brunswick, but also the oldest in Middlesex County. In 1827, Joseph and Jane Hoagland,[2] along with other local African Americans, most probably free, founded the church.[3] Islay had undoubtedly attended services there; now he would stand in the pulpit, intoning words of greeting and asking for the Lord's blessing, "May the words of my mouth and the meditation of my heart, be acceptable in thy sight, O Lord, my strength and my redeemer."[4]

Figure 1 Mt Zion AME Church Historical Marker

Graduation

Islay was about to make history as the first of two African American who officially graduated from the New Brunswick Seminary and were ordained by the Reformed Church in America.[5] Specifically, he was the first to be ordained by the "Classis of New Jersey."[6] There had been two Black candidates at the New Brunswick Theological Seminary, but the other student's (John Bergen) ordination was delayed because he had not yet found a mission or congregation in which to serve.

Islay knew there were no Reformed congregations that he could serve back home in Randolph County (North Carolina). Thus, he signed with the American Missionary Association (AMA). Members of that organization had long worked in the South, bringing education to African Americans, even before the end of slavery. He hoped eventually to serve in Nashville or Memphis, but first he would return to North Carolina.[7] Therefore, even though the two men, John Bergen and Islay, had graduated together, Islay would be the first ordained.

As one of the first two men of color to graduate from the prestigious New Brunswick Seminary, Walden and his upcoming ordination ceremony attracted a lot of attention. He was used to his activities being broadcast regularly by New Brunswick's *Daily Times*. The paper had followed every activity and accomplishment almost from the time he arrived in New Brunswick three years earlier. This time, however, it was not just the *Daily Times* reporting on his ordination. The *New York Evening Post* also took notice.

Evening Post

The *Evening Post*, a publication of William Cullen Bryant and Co., was published semiweekly between 1850 and 1919.[8] It was a notable publication. Bryant had been a well-known abolitionist before slavery ended. The reporter the *Post* sent to cover this momentous occasion asked questions not only about the ordination but also about Islay's background, his family, and his life in North Carolina. The article was titled "An Interesting Ordination."

Figure 2 An Interesting Ordination,
Evening Post

An Interesting Ordination
How Islay Walden, a Young Colored
Man Obtained His Education —
From Slavery to the Pulpit.
New Brunswick N.J., July 1, 1879.

The ordination of Islay Walden, a young colored man, took place in this city this afternoon, the laying on of hands having performed by the classis of New Jersey in the Second Reformed Church. Considerable interest was manifested in the ordination in the fact that Mr. Walden was the first colored man who was ever graduated of the theological seminary of the Reformed Church of America which is in this city, and from the fact that he is the first candidate from the colored race who has been ordained by the New Brunswick classis or any other classis in New Jersey.

Mr. Walden has had to struggle against apparently insurmountable difficulties to obtain an education. He was born in NC and he and his mother were several times sold as slaves. The price obtained for both when Walden was a babe in arms being $800. His father escaped from slavery by running away from his master and getting to Indiana on a forged passport. Young Walden was declared free when he was 22 years old and then he was ignorant of even the letters of the alphabet. At this age however, he formed a determination to become a teacher. He left home and traveled to Washington D.C., where, by force of his entreaties, he was allowed to enter Howard University. He remained there for more than six years and obtained a good education, notwithstanding that he was almost blind, defective vision being an infliction which came with his birth. After graduation at Howard University, he came north selling a small volume of poems of his own composition to obtain funds to pursue a theological education. He made applications to be admitted into the seminary at Princeton College, but Dr. McComb interposed some objection that very much disheartened Walden. He was more successful at New Brunswick, where Prof George W. Atherton of Rutgers College interested himself in his behalf and introduced him to the faculty at the theological seminary. About the time Walden was knocking at Prof Atherton's door, seeking an admission, the Rev. Dr. C.D. Hartranft, formerly of the Second Reformed Church of this city but now Professor of the Hartford Theological Seminary brought word that a member of the Rev. Dr. Coles' Reformed Church at Yonkers N.Y. had just left a legacy of $8500 for the education of a colored man. The Board of Education of the Reformed Church then took Mr. Walden under their care and he entered the theological seminary for three years course with another colored man named John R. Bergen. His innovation met with no opposition from the other students, but instead the utmost good feeling prevailed throughout the three years of his life there. The colored students although both suffered from defective vision kept their places in the classis and not infrequently distanced the white students in efficiency and aptness. They were both graduated last month and have been licensed to preach by the New Brunswick classis. Mr. Bergen will be ordained once his field of labor is decided upon. He has expressed a desire to go to Africa, but his physician thinks his constitution as not robust enough for that climate. Mr. Walden has been engaged by the American

Missionary Society to go south and labor among the freedmen. The Reformed Church has no missionaries in the south or Mr. Walden would have gone there under its auspices. At the ordination services this afternoon, the Rev. Dr. J.L. See, President of the Classis and Secretary of the Board of Education presided. The Rev J.M. Corwin, of Middlesex N.J., preached the services. The other clergymen who participated, were the Rev. Dr. W.H. Campbell, President of Rutgers College, the Rev. Dr. Lord of Metucheon NJ. The Rev. Messrs. Jacob Cooper and Doolittle of Rutgers College, the Rev. Dr. D.D. Demarest, Professor of Pastoral Theology and the theological seminary, and the Rev. Dr. Van Dyke of Hertzog Hall of this city. The Rev. Dr. Strieby, Secretary of the American Board of Missions was also present.[9]

It was a remarkable afternoon. After returning to his room, Islay reflected on the day's activities. He had come such a long way since leaving Randolph County, North Carolina, twelve years earlier. He accomplished so many things while away, overcome so many hurdles, some related to his blindness, some to his race, some to his financial struggles. He achieved so much in New Brunswick alone. The Student Mission he started was bursting at the seams. He told Dr. Demarest, a professor and dean, in a letter just the year before that they would need a larger facility. They had nearly outgrown the space at the seminary.[10] Now, he was leaving. In just a few days, he was headed back to North Carolina. The future of the Student Mission would be in the hands of the seminary. He could not help but reflect on how it all began.

Looking Back

In 1877, after obtaining his teaching degree, Islay returned to New Jersey, a place he spent time before attending Howard University. He hoped to attend Princeton's theological seminary, but Princeton had not been accommodating. The school was not willing to admit an African American student. However, with the help of George Washington Atherton, a renowned history and political science professor from Rutgers (who would go on to be president of Penn State University[11]), scholarship monies had been found for Islay to attend New Brunswick Theological Seminary. He would need additional funds, though, for room and board and various sundry items. In particular, he needed a reader, someone who could help him read his textbooks, take notes, and so on. He was, after all, nearly blind. He was able to walk about. He could see some light and shapes from behind his clouded cataracts. He'd been this way since birth, so he had been able to perform his duties while enslaved. His ability to function in low light, to rely on other senses, had served him well while working the gold mines of the Uwharrie Mountains in North Carolina. He'd even been able to walk to Washington, D.C., in the late 1860s, but reading was another matter. He had an excellent memory, but someone had to read the information to him first. He had done it before. He relied heavily on his memory to learn the lecture materials that others read to him and then delivered to audiences eager to pay.[12]

In reflecting back, he would have to say that his life in Washington D.C. had been good. He arrived in the winter of 1867–68 not knowing anyone. He had walked from his home in Randolph County. Despite leaving Randolph County in the warmth of late summer, cooler weather had come by the time he arrived in Raleigh. He would stay with Walden cousins there, the John Chavis Walden family.[13] His stopover in Raleigh would also mean he would have to earn some money before continuing his journey north, to the nation's capital, the city from which President Lincoln had issued the Emancipation Proclamation that declared him free. He also found companionship there. However, despite marrying Amelia Frances "Fannie" Harriss in October 1867,[14] while still in Raleigh, he arrived in Washington alone. Apparently, he never mentioned her to anyone. The author has found no additional information about her to date.

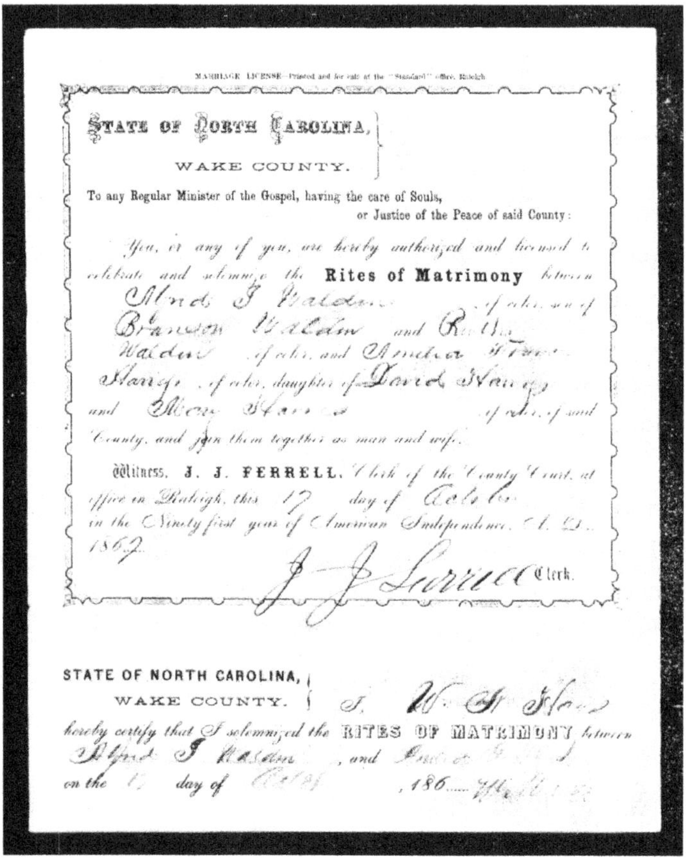

Figure 3 Marriage record of (Alfred) Islay Walden and Amelia Frances Harriss, 17 October 1867, Wake County, North Carolina

The War Was Over

Islay heard the news that the war was over, and he was free, from his last enslaver, Jesse Smitherman. Smitherman owned large farms, with a large, enslaved workforce, in Montgomery County, North Carolina, next door to Randolph County. However, Islay was born enslaved by James Garner, in Randolph County, not just Islay, but his mother, Ruth; his sister, Sarah; and possibly his father, Branson, as well. When James Garner died, Islay, Ruth, and Sarah, were bought from the estate by James's son Dolphin Garner. A man named "Brantly" on James Garner's estate inventory may have been Islay's father, Branson. He was sold to Eli Moffitt.[15] Islay told the *New York Evening Post* that his father had escaped west, becoming self-emancipated, but there is no additional information. At some unidentified point, Jesse Smitherman acquired Islay.

With the war over, Islay set out for Washington, D.C. His hopes were high that he could get an education and find someone who might be able to help him to see better. The trip to Washington was arduous. According to C.C. Harper, in his introduction to *Miscellaneous Poems*, "He came on foot, the snow falling during part of the journey."[16]

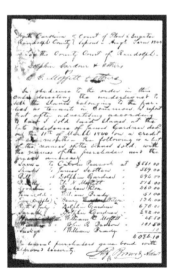

Figure 4 Sale of Slaves, Estate of James Gardner, August Term 1844,
Court of Common Pleas & Quarter Sessions, Randolph County, North Carolina

A Visit to Philadelphia

Islay had only been in Washington a few months when the excitement of General Ulysses S. Grant being the Republican nominee for president overwhelmed the country and especially the city of Washington, D.C. The Pennsylvania Republican Convention was being held in March 1868 in Philadelphia. Not only were people from all over Pennsylvania converging on the city hoping to watch the proceedings, but also many of the soldiers and sailors who had fought in the war and felt he was their leader now headed to Philadelphia so they could cheer for their hero, so they could see history made yet again. Islay was excited to join them, excited to see history made by the man he credited for his freedom.

The Philadelphia Convention

The convention was called to order by Colonel Frank Jordan, chairman of the State Central Committee. The resolution to nominate Grant was filled with heady optimism:

Resolved, *That by the election of General Grant to the Presidency, all domestic dissention and factious opposition to the complete reconstruction of the Union on the firm foundations laid by the wise and judicious legislation of Congress will be immediately suppressed and harmony and good feeling restored — settled relations of business established and the revival and improvement of all the disturbed sources of national wealth and prosperity will be secured, when it is once made manifest that the people of this country are firmly fixed in the determination that the fruits of the late bloody and obstinate struggle shall not be lost, and that the factious and rebellious resistance to the laws shall be as effectually overthrown as was the military hostility which attempted to subvert the Government by savage cruelty, rapine, and murder.*[17]

The Dunlaps

Islay was exhilarated by the events of the day and evening. He had only a small amount of money left at the end of the day. Unfortunately, he lost his return train ticket sometime during the day's events, perhaps due to a pickpocket. That wasn't the end of his bad luck. In an essay, he stated he was abandoned by his traveling companions. Without money for a room or bed in a guesthouse, he planned to stay in a coal bin along the wharf; however, his luck was about to change.

While walking down Broad Street, two men passed him chatting with each other. Islay overheard them refer to him as a "carpetbagger." First excusing himself for eavesdropping, Islay politely explained that carpetbaggers didn't come from the South. The men were intrigued. They stopped and questioned him about where he was from. One of the men, William Dunlap, was apparently taken with his story and invited him back to his home. Islay accepted gratefully. After dinner, the family sat listening to his life story. Then, after ending the evening with prayers, Islay was invited to stay over. He described his room as a "striking contrast" to the coal bin where he thought he would be sleeping:[18]

On awaking in the morning, I found myself in so different a place from what I had anticipated, that I was at a loss to determine whether I was awake or dreaming....The floor was nicely carpeted; the bed made of feathers and dressed with rose-bordered blankets, and a snow-ball counterpane, with pillows as soft as downy pillows are. There was a large spring-bottomed rocking-chair, a bowl and pitcher, a bureau with a large mirror on it, and many other things which augmented the comfort and happiness of its fortunate occupant.[19]

The Dunlaps, intrigued by their new friend, invited him to spend several days. "I remained with them until Wednesday, at which time, being supplied with passage money, I left for Washington."[20]

Who were these generous people, the Dunlaps? There is no definitive information, but Islay gave us some hints in his description of his encounter and stay with them. William Dunlap was "one of the leading men of Philadelphia in the anti-slavery movement, and a just man."[21] He was most likely a cotton fabric merchant, born in Ireland, and married to Rebecca with two young children, William Jr. and Eliza.[22] Although Islay stated that Dunlap was involved in the antislavery movement, there is no indication from anything Islay wrote (or anything found by this writer) that the Dunlaps were Quakers.

Islay mentioned Dunlap's two small children, William and Eliza, who "although very young, looked upon me with purely angelic faces, and before the evening passed I became the centre [sic] of attraction."[23] He noted that Eliza was the only child at the reception for Grant that the general kissed, saying, "For she's the child he gave a kiss."[24] Islay dedicated a poem to her as part of his honorific for William Dunlap and family. It is not clear to what reception Islay is referring. Grant was not reported as attending the Philadelphia convention, nor was there any reception for him reported to be held afterward. Did he slip in and out of town, under the radar, unbeknownst to the press? It would seem so based on Islay's poem. A few days later, Islay returned to Washington, D.C. The Dunlaps generously gave him money for his trip back to Washington.

Back in Washington, D.C.

Inaugurations have traditionally included an open house at the White House. Grant's, in 1869, was no different. Islay was excited at the opportunity to see his hero. In a letter to his niece Catherine Hill, he mentioned a poem that he wrote and gave to the president:

When I was about giving up all hopes of getting an education, I visited President Grant, and after talking to him a while, I pulled out a copy of a little poem which I composed, which I presented to him on bidding him good-bye. He gave me a warm shake of that heroic hand which so materially aided in emancipating four millions [sic] of slaves, crushing the rebellion, and is now so successfully binding the heart of every American to his country's cause, and said, "Never pause until you become educated." Such words, coming from such a source, to an uncultivated mind, indeed left impressions that time only can efface.[25]

The advice was fortuitous. A year later, Islay would begin his pursuit of funds for his education in earnest.

A Witness to History

On April 2, 1870, Islay and thousands of those formerly enslaved would have their wildest dreams realized. That day, the Fifteenth Amendment was ratified, giving them the right to vote. This was the last of the amendments that would make those (men) formerly enslaved fully enfranchised citizens. The Thirteenth Amendment ended slavery (with some interesting caveats); the Fourteenth Amendment declared those formerly enslaved to be full citizens; and now the Fifteenth Amendment gave formerly enslaved men full voting rights! The *New Age*, for which Frederick Douglass was the corresponding editor and Stella Martin, Esq., was editor, ran an article on the amendment's impending ratification on February 10, 1870, called "The Fifteenth Amendment."[26] It began with a provocative and potentially incendiary statement: "Good riddance to the negro!"

For two hundred and fifty years he has been a thorn in the flesh. The Fifteenth Amendment has extracted him....Shades of the slaves of Jamestown haunt us no more! Let the blood of Crispus Attucks cry no more from the ground as the consecrating libation of our revolution against the nation that held his descendants in slavery. Thou old Saint, hero and martyr of Harper's Ferry, let thy soul betake itself to rest! We have followed thy marching on to the end of battle and the day of victory.

Two months later, reports of celebrations from around the country were published. Washington, D.C.'s *Evening Star* summarized the day's events in the nation's capital:[27]

THE FIFTEENTH AMENDMENT — The colored people of the United States, deeming it fit and proper that some suitable demonstration should be made to express their gratification at the ratification of the fifteenth amendment to the constitution of the United States, authorized the national executive committee to issue a proclamation announcing the termination of this important event and today (Saturday, April 2d) being the anniversary of the fall of Richmond and the death knell of the rebellion, the committee have decided on this day as appropriate for carrying out the provisions as ordered. In accordance therewith a national salute was fired at 12m.

And also for the national executive committee in the name of the colored people of the United States, to select Sunday, April 3d, at 11 a. m. precisely, as the time for an oration to be delivered at Israel Church, Capital [sic] Hill, Stella Martin, Esq., to be the orator of the day, George T. Downing, president, and Prof. George P. Vashon, to be poet of the occasion.

Islay, like hundreds of others, was there. While passing through the crowd, a young girl, Clara Saunders, noticed his eyes and took his hand to lead him across the street in safety. It was a chance meeting; he did not know her. Nevertheless, he wrote a poem to express his gratitude. In it, he indicated that she was very young, referring to her repeatedly as a child. This poem is one of the few times he references his compromised eyesight.[28]

Behold the great and swelling crowd,
While thronging through the street,
And then behold the hand that keeps
Me from the horses feet.
The great and small have passed me by,
And here unseen I stand;
I have no sympathy no help,
Except this little hand.
And now I bless this little hand,
Which gently takes my arm;
Kind Jesus, guide this little child,
And keep her from all harm.
The proud and gay are passing by,
And foolishly have scorned,

When they have met me on the street
Afflicted as when born.
But now and then I meet a child
As harmless as a dove,
Who tells me by its little deeds,
That God alone is love.
Dear Saviour, bless this little child,
Whate'er her name may be;
Dost Thou not see her little heart,
How kind she's been to me!

It may be that Islay did not know this girl's name at the time he wrote the poem. The introduction wherein he names her was probably written in 1872, when he was collecting his poems/letters in anticipation of publication. By then, Clara Saunders was a student in Class D, in the Model School program of the Normal Department at Howard University.[29]

Once the Fifteenth Amendment was ratified, the First Ward Republicans had assembled at the Stevens School in Northwest Washington to finalize arrangements for a serenade of the president in front of the White House in gratitude. At the White House, the president, vice president. and others gathered, including Charles Sumner, Republican senator from Massachusetts, who would introduce a civil rights bill calling for equal rights in all areas of public life. On this night, Sumner's comments included remarks on education, which the *Evening Star* reported:

Figure 5 Charles Sumner

21

REMARKS OF MR. SUMNER.

Mr. Sumner commenced by congratulating them on the great results accomplished in securing equal rights for all, which for years had been his hope and object—to see the promise of the Declaration of Independence become a reality. [Cheers.] He would not say that it was entirely accomplished, for it is not. It was his nature to think more of what remains to be done than of what has been done—more of duties than of triumphs. He had only just heard from Philadelphia of a decision in a court of justice that a colored person of foreign birth could not be naturalized in this country because of color. This is in accordance with an old statute—a relic of the days of slavery. He had now a bill before the Judiciary Committee of the Senate striking the word white from our naturalization laws. It remains further that equal rights shall be received in all the public conveyances in the United States, that no one be excluded therefrom by reason of color. It also remains, he said, that you here in Washington shall complete this equality of rights in your common schools. You all go together to vote, and any person may find a seat in the Senate of the United States, but the child is shut out of the common school on account of color. This discrimination must be abolished. All schools must be open to all without distinction of color. In accomplishing this you will work, not only for yourselves, but will set an example for all the land, and most especially for the South. Only in this way can your school system be extended for the equal good of all; and now, as you have at heart the education of your children, that they should grow up in that knowledge of equal rights, so essential for their protection to the world, it is your bounden duty here in Washington to see that this is accomplished. Your school system must be founded on equal rights, so that no one shall be excluded on account of color. [Applause.]

At the close of Mr. Sumner's speech, several airs were played, and the assemblage then proceeded to the north end of the Arlington Hotel, and Col. Fremont was next called upon. The committee were introduced to the Colonel, who thanked them for the compliment tendered him. After an interchange of salutations they retired, the Colonel declining to address them on account of indisposition. Secretary Fish was next called upon at his residence, and Secretary Boutwell was found to be there on a visit. Secretary Fish, after thanking the citizens for the compliment paid him, and expressing his regret that they had not a better night for the demonstration, then introduced the Secretary of the Treasury.

Figure 6 Remarks of Mr. Charles Sumner, 2 April 1870, at the celebration of the 15th Amendment.

...It also remains, he said, that you here in Washington shall complete this equality of rights in your common schools. You all go together to vote, and any person may find a seat in the Senate of the United States, but the child is shutout on account of color. This discrimination must be abolished. All schools must be open to all without distinction of color. In accomplishing this you will work, not only for yourselves, but will set an example for all the land, and most especially for the South. Only in this way can your school system be extended for the equal good of all; and now, as you have at heart the education of your children, that they should grow up in that knowledge of equal rights, so essential to their protection to the world, it is your bounden duty here in Washington to see that this is accomplished. Your school system must be founded on equal rights, so that no one will be excluded on account of color.[30]

Although Islay left us no direct report of the day's celebrations, he echoes Sumner in a poem called "The Nation's Friend,"[31] In it, he refers to an anticipated national brotherhood where there would be education for all:

> *Where we may have our public schools,*
> *With open doors displayed;*
> *Where all may drink at wisdom's fount*
> *With none to make afraid.*
> *Young friends, I know you will be there*
> *Bright, shining, as the sun;*
> *With equal rights secured to all,*
> *When Sumner's work is done.*
> *The nation's friend! Still firm he stands,*
> *With neither sleep nor slumber,*
> *Come every Freedman in this land*
> *And hail the name of Sumner.*[32]

Islay may not have realized it then, but it would not be long before he would begin his own education.

Seeking an Education

In September 1870, notices appeared in the newspaper in Wilmington, Delaware, requesting that the person who "ordered printing for a lecture by Islay Walden, please call and settle the bill."[33] It is difficult to know if Islay was headed north making his way to New Jersey or returning to Washington, D.C., delivering lectures along the way, most likely for a fee. Islay was determined to find a way to get an education. He was not going to be discouraged by those who said he was too old or those who said his vision was too impaired.

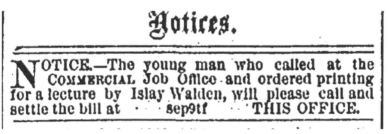

Figure 7 Wilmington Daily Commercial, Wilmington, Delaware, 9 September 1870

Islay did have those who were encouraging and supportive. One such person was the Reverend Dr. Danforth B. Nichols of Howard University, whom he met at a "preaching service."[34] Professor Nichols was one of the original faculty members of Howard University, a professor in biblical history and geography and the former superintendent of the Freedmen's Village, in Arlington, Virginia.[35] Nichols and his daughter, Sarah, were very supportive of Islay's efforts to get an education. Sarah was one of his first teachers, helping him learn to read. (It is unknown how he overcame his vision deficiencies.)[36] He acknowledged the contributions of both Dr.

Nichols and his daughter in his poetry. Of Dr. Nichols, whom he called his "Benefactor," he wrote,

> *It's true I have a friend, indeed,*
> *Whom I can safely trust and heed;…*
> *He found me in a seeking state,*
> *And placed me here among the great….*
> *I came to him when much oppressed,*
> *And soon he eased my troubled breast;*
> *And now I bless the way he led,*
> *When all my sorrows quickly fled.*[37]

Of Sarah Nichols he wrote,

> *Sarah, thy name shall ever live!*
> *Shall have the best place in my heart,*
> *For the instruction though [sic] didst give,*
> *When others bade me to depart….*[38]

Figure 8 Danforth B. Nichols

North to New Jersey

Encouragement from Dr. Nichols and Sarah was not enough. Islay still needed funds to be able to further his education. Thus, he headed north, giving lectures, and selling poetry along the way, eventually arriving in New Brunswick, New Jersey. Exactly what led him to New Brunswick is not clear, but Islay's stay there was surprisingly successful, according to C.C. Harper.

While in New Jersey he attracted the attention of the Second Reformed Church in New Brunswick, which, through Professor Atherton, pledged one hundred and fifty dollars a year toward his school expenses until he should graduate.[39]

Professor George Atherton was born in Massachusetts, the son of a farmer and cotton mill owner. He was a graduate of Yale University, a captain in the Union army, and had earned his law degree. Atherton taught at the Albany (New York) Academy and University of Illinois before going to Rutgers as a political science professor. He would stay there until 1882, when he became president of Pennsylvania State University.[40]

With the scholarship Islay received, thanks to Atherton, he was able to begin formal studies at Howard University. According to school catalogs, he was in the Model School program,[41] which was intended to prepare students to enter either the Normal Department, a three-year teacher preparation program, or the Preparatory Department, where students were prepared to attend any four-year college program.[42]

Figure 9 Professor George W. Atherton

In 1872, then a student at Howard, Islay wrote a letter to Professor Atherton expressing his appreciation and gratitude.

Howard University,
Washington, D.C., Dec. 13, 1972

Dear Sir: Two years will soon have passed since my connection with this University, and I am happy to say I am progressing finely; and am rapidly approaching my sixth examination, at which time every energy shall be bent to its utmost extreme. I have been making out my expenses which I find to be very heavy, though not to be compared with the small amount of knowledge which I have gained; and, too, when I consider that these privileges of going to school have partially grown out of your influence, I am constrained to express my gratitude to you. I should have made an acknowledgment ere this, but thought it best to wait until I am sufficiently competent; and would still wait longer — [43]

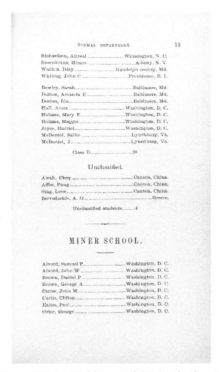

Figure 10 Islay Walden, Model School, Class D,
Normal Department, Howard University, 1871

Advocacy

Islay would visit New Brunswick frequently over the next few years. He was in New Jersey in the summer of 1871, when the *Trenton State Journal* published a notice that he was a student in the Model School, in the Normal Department at Howard University, and would be trying to raise money for his continued education.[44] He spent at least part of the summer of 1872 in New Brunswick. He referenced his stay in a letter he wrote in October 1872, to the Reverend Dr. Chester D. Hartranft. Dr. Hartranft (misspelled in *Miscellaneous Poems* as "Hartraught") was pastor of the Second Reformed Church in New Brunswick and a professor at the New Brunswick Theological Seminary.[45] In his letter, Islay referenced his experiences attending "Sabbath school, prayer meetings, and other religious worship."[46] Based on letters he wrote in August and September, it appeared he met individuals during those activities for whose admission to Howard he would advocate.

Figure 11 Chester D. Hartranft

In August, Islay wrote a letter to Emma Crane, assistant in charge of the Model School, in the Normal Department at Howard University.[47] Emma Crane was not only someone he knew as an administrator, but also someone he referred to as a friend that he found to be "just and true."[48] In typical poetic style, he speaks of his pen as a friend and goes on to talk about the many things it can do. Using this literary device, he then pleads the case of a Miss Johnson.

It knows a maid both just and true,
One weighed in virtue's scale,
Whom I will now present to you,
Whose deeds can never fail.
A student she would gladly be,
She has no means nor friend
Who freely would, that she can see,
For her a dollar spend
Oh! Lay her case before the east,
Or thy own native State,
That they may take her from the least,
And place her with the great.
Tell them, for me, their name shall live
With thine on history's page,
If they Miss Johnson aid will give,
The fair one of this age....
Remember, that her parents died
When she was but a child.
She has no lovers by her side,
Though she is meek and mild.

In September, Islay wrote to the faculty of Howard University, while he was in Philadelphia.[49] Again, he speaks about his pen.

Gentlemen, I my pen have raised,
The one by which your Board I've praised;...
It is a pen I long have trained....
For truly it does speak today,...
Remember that its highest aim is much like yours – is much the same; ...
Therefore I place upon its wings
The name of her who plays and sings,
And all thy honors I'll extend
If you will be this singer's friend....
In every song your name she'll praise,
If you will crown her student days.

In the next paragraph/stanza, he turns to advocating for additional individuals.

I hope that you'll accept of me,
Not only one, but names of three;
And then excuse these lines I write,
For one is dark and two are white.
Behold their names I did omit,
For them there is no place as yet,
Therefore it's well each one knows,
that I can send their names in prose.

Here he seemed to be recommending one African American student and two white students. At the end of the letter, he indicated, by requesting school catalogs, that he hoped to encourage others to attend Howard.

Ten catalogues I hope you'll send
For here four days I have to spend,
To me send them by the Express,
For now I have not my address. …

There's no information on whether Miss Johnson or any of the other three individuals for whom he advocated ever attended Howard.

Life at Howard

Despite his visual deficiencies, Islay made short work of the preparatory program in the Model School. By 1873, he was a full student in the Normal Department.[50] Three years later, he graduated. He had gone from being completely illiterate to a teaching degree from the Normal Department at Howard University in six years. Notice of his graduation had been published in the newspapers, including the topic of his graduation essay, "A Glance at Science."[51] However, life had not been easy when he first arrived at Howard.

Islay had no real resources when he started Howard. He had obtained a scholarship to attend school, but he needed money to survive, for housing and food. He'd been known to give public recitations of poems and ballads. After he learned to read and write, he had committed his poems to paper. With encouragement from J.L.H. Winfield, from the War Department and C.C. Harper, a founder of the American Colonization Society, he would use his newly published volume of poems to help obtain the monies needed to support himself. His little volume, *Miscellaneous Poems which the Author Dedicated to the Cause of Education and Humanity*, was well received. Its publication was announced around the country, in such places as Chicago, Illinois;[52] Harrisburg, Pennsylvania;[53] Redwing, Minnesota;[54] Redwood Falls, Minnesota;[55] Rockford, Illinois;[56] and New York, New York.[57] In Brooklyn (then a separate city from New York City), the *Brooklyn Daily Eagle* published a notice about Islay's visit:

Islay Walden, a student of Howard University, Washington, and now visiting this city, has published a volume of poems, religious, secular and miscellaneous. The author is heartily commended by Professor A. Barber and other people of the Federal Capital.[58]

People were not used to thinking of "a young colored man" sharing poetry.

Islay was writing down his poetry as soon as he learned to read and write. In June 1872, he wrote in a letter to Dr. See, secretary of the Reformed Church in America, that he had written over thirty additional poems and was planning to publish a small volume of his poems (*Miscellaneous Poems*).

Dr. See:

Dear Friend: I should have written you before, but being very busy in my studies, I have been putting it off until I should have time....

I am doing very well in my studies, and have found time, in connection with them, to attend about half of the Theological lectures. During this year I have composed about thirty poems. I am going to have a book published this summer, which I hope will meet a favorable consideration from the reading public.[59]

It appears from that letter he was already thinking seriously about pursuing theological studies, but that would have to wait.

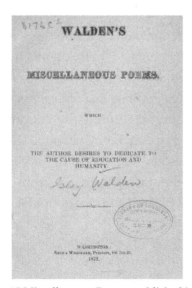

Figure 12 Miscellaneous Poems, published in 1873

The Literary Society

Islay's references to Howard University always seemed to be positive. However, he did have a dispute with the Junior Literary Society.[60] The dispute was serious enough for him to resign his membership. In his letter to the society, he explained that he wished to apologize for what he perceived as his inappropriate behavior. However, he was clear that he was not apologizing for what he believed were justified remarks, nor was he asking to be reinstated. This letter was uncharacteristically strident.

> *Think not I come to curry favor,*
> *For that would be beneath my aim,*
> *And I would crucify my honor,*
> *And put my manhood thus to shame.*
> *I merely come to right the crooked,*
> *To make amends where I was wrong....*
> *I must confess through heat of passion,*
> *Your president I did offend,...*

Islay then turns to clearly accuse the society of what he believes is their wrongdoing.

> *You, ravening, wolf like, would devour*
> *And swallow me up heels and head, ...*

However, he retorts,

> *Your nets my feet shall never tangle,*
> *Nor will I tread your winding way,*
> *True courtesy among you Juniors*
> *Is what I long have sought to gain,*
> *In spite of all my humble efforts,*
> *My work to me seems all is vain.*
> *Therefore, it's best that we should sever,*
> *Before another rising sun,*

That each may in this fleeting contest
Think that he has the victory won....
I'd freely give up my tuition,
Or give to you my heart and hand,
If we could live in union severed,
Or else within this happy band....
Perhaps from this we'll take a warning,
May learn to be both just and kind.
Therefore, I bid you happy Juniors,
A mournful, long and last farewell,...

Of course, he did not give up his tuition.

Women Friends

His dispute with the Literary Society notwithstanding, Islay did have friends. He referenced them in his writings. While most of the men he mentioned seemed to be mentors, in contrast, the women he wrote about were mostly classmates, objects of his affection and admiration. They were not all romantic, but they seemed meaningful. Was he a ladies' man? There is no real evidence of that, but he clearly had a respect and fondness for the women around him.

Figure 13 (L) Main Hall & (R) Miner Hall,
Howard University, 1868

Islay wrote about a young woman at Miner Hall who was headed back to Miner after dinner in the main Dining Hall. It was raining, so he sought to escort her and possibly share his umbrella or coat against the elements. Somehow there was a misunderstanding when another student made a comment that "they" would be fine. The student (unnamed) meant someone else, not the woman to whom he was speaking. Poor Islay, embarrassed, turned away, apparently to the surprise of the young lady he hoped to escort, a "Miss W*****." True to form, he wrote a poem of apology, saying,

> *Therefore you were not slighted,*
> *Not in the least degree;*
> *Although, when not a thinking,*
> *I turned aside from thee....*
> *Therefore, you will excuse me,*
> *For I have made it plain,*
> *And sorry that I left you,*
> *Last night within the rain....*
> *Now, when the night grows darker,*
> *And rain shall harder fall,...*
> *Or when the moon is shining,*
> *And stars shall fill the sky,*
> *I will not then forsake you,*
> *Nor let you pass me by.*[61]

Although Islay never named this young woman, she might have been Margaret M. Wright, a student from Washington, D.C., in the Miner School in 1872.[62]

Figure 14 General Oliver Otis Howard

Islay had also made friends with a Native American classmate. In October 1872, that friendship compelled Islay to write a poem wherein he would answer in the affirmative the question, "Can the Indian be Civilized and Christianized?" This was a time when the so-called Indian Wars were being fought in the West. In fact, General O.O. Howard, founding president of Howard University and the one for whom the university was named, had played a prominent role in those campaigns. In a poem written in honor of Howard, called "Ode to Gen. O.O. Howard," Islay had a different view of Native Americans, saying that Howard was

> *...in a heathen land,*
> *Where red-men may around him stand,*
> *With tomahawk and scalping knife,*
> *And threaten vengeance on his life.*[63]

However, in the 1872 poem, "Dedicated to a Young Lady," Islay did not reference his earlier attitudes, but indicated that he believed now that Native people could be "civilized" based on his personal interactions with this young Native American woman.

> *...It's true that I often write of Queens,*
> *And those of noble fame;*
> *But now I seek to write a line,*
> *Upon thy honored name.*
> *What's in thy name moves me to write,*
> *This little verse to thee?*
> *Perhaps it is thy pleasant ways,*
> *And cheering looks to me.*
> *How oft I think of thee, kind Miss,*
> *And oft admire thy grace,*
> *Because I know that thou art of*
> *Another noble race!*

As the poem continues, it becomes apparent that the two were flirting, or at least he was flirting with her.[64] There is no indication that anything more ever developed, nor did he ever name this young woman. The only name found in the catalogs during this time was Alson D. Bemo, from Marshalltown, Indian Territory.[65]

Marshalltown was a town located in the Creek/Muskogee Nation.[66] However, Marshalltown was known as an African American town that was founded at the end of the Civil War for those formerly enslaved by the indigenous enslavers in the Five Civilized tribes. The Bemo name was and is found principally among those in the Creek and Seminole Nations. Was it possible that Islay's classmate was a "Black Indian," as mixed African American and Native Americans have come to be identified? Marshalltown no longer exists. Interestingly, none of Islay's other poems reference Native Americans.

In April 1873, Islay was keen to begin a pen pal correspondence with a Virginia Delaney. There is no indication from his letter or poem where this young woman was living or where he met her. In contrast to others, she did not seem to be a classmate. However, he implored her to begin an ongoing correspondence. It appeared he was quite smitten with Virginia.

For this my pen has long displayed,
E'er long its been delighted,
To know thou art a fair young maid
Whom no one yet has slighted....
Remember that I'm full of pride,
Of pity and compassion,
And she who lingers by my side
Should like my style and fashion....
Kind Miss, to thee no more I'll say,
Nor add unto my measure,
Except to write without delay
When it may be your pleasure.[67]

Islay never said if Virginia wrote to him. However, she may have been the "Miss V" of another poem.

> Go tell Miss V** to quickly come,
> And bring her pen and ink.
> That she may write each word I speak
> Or each on that I think.
> She can unfold my darkest thoughts
> And make them plain to me,
> I know not one so full of art
> No one so apt as she.
> She was with me on first of May;
> For me she then did write
> With little kind and gentle deeds,
> She's like my heart's delight.[68]

Islay did not just write poems professing his attraction for the women in his life. He also encouraged their endeavors, such as two young women whose sewing skills he praised. One poem was dedicated to "M.W.W.," when she made her first shirt.

> Mary, my shirt is neatly made,
> Each stitch is in its proper place,
> There's not a wrinkle to be seen,
> Nor basting thread that will deface....
> I think I see within it stitched,
> A figure of your daily life;
> It surely tells that you will make,
> Some happy man a thrifty wife.
> And now I speak unto the hand,
> That never made a shirt before: --
> Work hard to cultivate the mind,
> Then arduous tasks will soon be o'er.[69]

Islay's comments about marriage probably would not be considered complimentary in the twenty-first century. There is no way to know what Miss M.W.W. thought of them. Miss M.W.W. may have been Mary W. Warrick in Class A of the Model School in 1872.[70]

The second poem references a Miss S****.

> *My shirt is truly neat and strong*
> *Although for it I waited long;*
> *I know Miss S**** will never slight,*
> *Nor sew on shirts by candle light.*
> *I long have known this one who sews,*
> *And now commend her to her beaux,*
> *She has no artificial ways*
> *To cause young men on her to gaze.*[71]

Clearly, Miss S**** was not an object of his affection, but was someone he had "long" known, suggesting she entered the program at Howard about the same time. As for the "artificial ways" that would cause "young men on her to gaze," Islay seemed to be implying that she was not overly flirtatious. Rather typical for Victorian-era men, he was always exceedingly concerned with respecting a woman's virtue. Miss S**** may have been his classmate Victoria Shaw.[72]

Ultimately, Islay did not find a permanent relationship with any of the women he admired at Howard. That would wait for another time. First, he would finish his education at Howard and then seek ordination and the ministry. Only then would he turn to find a wife.

The Sabbath School

While a student in Washington, Islay established a Sabbath school. Sabbath schools were important to the education of the formerly enslaved. Besides the schools run by the Freedmen's Bureau, there were church-sponsored Sabbath schools and night schools that taught basic literacy skills. These schools were run by and for African Americans, children and adults alike.[73] It appears Islay's school was begun sometime in 1872, when he penned a poem soliciting fellow students and teachers to help him establish the school.

Oh! Hark unto this liberal call;
For you are all invited,
And if you stay away I know,
The children will be slighted.
Oh! Why not come into the school –
For you may be a teacher;
Of all the beauties of the day,
This is the brightest future....[74]

Others from the university did help, professors and students. Looking at the roster of his classmates in the Normal program at Howard, it is not hard to picture some of them helping to teach. For example, one of his fellow students was Thomas Van Renssalaer Gibbs.[75]

Thomas Van Renssalaer Gibbs

Thomas Gibbs was the son of the Reverend Jonathan Clarkson Gibbs II, an African American politician. Thomas would also serve in the Florida State House of Representatives, where he and his father would help ensure the passage of legislation that established the State Normal College for Colored Students in 1887, which would eventually become the notable Florida Agricultural and Mechanical University (FAMU). Thomas would serve as principal and vice president of the school, whose home was in Tallahassee. There is a personal connection to this. The author's paternal grandmother, Lela Virginia Farnell (Williams), was one of the first students at this Florida school. Thomas Gibbs's wife, a teacher at the Normal School, signed Lela's autograph book.[76] Islay would be the founder of the church and school in North Carolina that would serve members of the author's maternal family for generations.[77]

Figure 15 Thomas Van Renssalaer Gibbs

As the school got underway, Islay offered a prayer for those gathered:

Jesus my Saviour and my King,
Oh, Grant this school a song to sing,
That we together here may meet,
And bow and worship at thy feet.

And when we shall have left this place,
Then give us of thy richest grace,
And lead each one unto his home,
That we may praise thee on thy throne!

> *And if we here shall meet no more,*
> *Then let us meet on Canaan's shore,*
> *Where we may walk the streets around,*
> *And wear a robe and starry crown.*[78]

The Sabbath school was very successful. Islay did not know it then, but eight years after his death and sixteen years after leaving Washington, D.C., his efforts would be remembered still.

Islay Walden, an odd genius, poet and preacher, during his collegiate days at Howard University, some twenty odd years ago, conducted a very well attended non-denominational Sunday school here. The teachers, young men and women, were drawn from the departments and the University. The singing of the school was a most attractive feature.[79]

Among the singers mentioned was a man who would become the renowned journalist John Edward Bruce, known as Bruce Grit, who may have been a student at Howard University in this period.[80] According to the *Washington Bee* report, Bruce's bass voice "could always be heard distinctly above all others, those days when the skill of his right hand had not been so universally acknowledged."[81]

Figure 16 John Edward Bruce

45

Bruce was familiar undoubtedly with Islay's poetry. In 1911, he and Arthur A. Schomburg would include the "Poems of Islay Walden, blind poet of North Carolina," in the original collection of the Negro Society for Historical Research, now known as the Schomburg Center for Research in Black Culture, in New York City.[82] Notices announcing this research society appeared in papers around the country, including in the *Pittsburgh Courier*,[83] the *Lexington Standard*,[84] and Franklin's *The Statesman*.[85]

A Spiritual Calling

Islay's writings exposed his two passions: education and love of God. While his poems in *Sacred Hymns* are clearly spiritual, there are many in *Miscellaneous Poems*, along with other statements, that illuminate his strong faith and deeply personal relationship with God. In answer to today's question often heard in evangelical circles, "Do you have a personal relationship with God?" Islay openly affirms in his poetry that he did. He refers to "Jesus, My Friend."[86] He says in "Doubts and Fears," that Jesus "scatters doubts and fear."[87] He even questions why he ever had any doubt in the poem titled "My Refuge."[88] Perhaps the clearest declaration of his sense of religious vocation is in his poem, "Consecration of Self."[89]

> *Jesus, I feel the quickening spark,*
> *O how it burns within!*
> *'Tis love that purifies the heart,*
> *And cleanses from all sin.*
> *And now I stretch my hands to Thee;*
> *Dear Saviour bid me fly,*
> *That I may in thy presence be,*
> *And reign above the sky.*
> *Where I may wear a starry crown,*
> *Through ceaseless years to come,*
> *And in the city I'll be found,*
> *Around thy dazzling throne.*

Although some may read this as a desire for death, it is more likely an expression of a deep desire for spiritual union, expressed in eschatological language.

Islay's concern for the spiritual well-being and educational opportunities of those back home in Randolph County is evident in a letter he wrote to his niece Catherine in April 1872.[90] Noting that she told him that she, her mother, and her aunt, had "professed religion" and "joined the church," he said that he was "lead to weep" when he read the news.[91] By the same token, he said he was "gratified to know that the letter which you sent me was written by your own dear little hand."[92] However, he also replied to her comments about wishing for "such privileges" as he enjoys, that he wished that she might be able to "study and do more good for the poor children in your neighborhood in the way of teaching them." He went on to say, "I sympathize with you much, and were I able you should not pant for learning any longer but should come even here and drink from the same well of knowledge out of which I draw daily."[93] Nevertheless, the one lesson he wanted her to understand was the one he believed he had learned, which was,

It is better to trust in God than in the promises of mankind, though some men are really instruments for good in His hands, all along the winding ways of life, to point us to a higher station than that in which we are placed, even by circumstances.[94]

It was that faith that would lead him back to New Jersey and the New Brunswick Theological Seminary. It was his love of family and community that would eventually lead him back to Randolph County, to be their teacher and pastor.

New Brunswick

Islay may have been turned down by Princeton's theological school, but he was neither discouraged nor deterred. He had close ties with the Reformed Church in America from his earliest days in the North. Exactly how he was introduced to the various Reformed clergy who ultimately befriended him and became his patrons is unclear. It is apparent that he was frequently a guest in their homes and their congregations.

I Love the Great Reformed

As mentioned previously, Islay wrote a letter to Dr. See, secretary of the Reformed Church. As part of that letter, he included a poem that speaks of his love for the Reformed Church.

Figure 17 An 1883 Engraving by John Minton, a New York City Engraver, of New Brunswick Theological Seminary

Doctor, I love the great Reformed

And pause within her arms; …
Her millions she has landed safe,

Upon fair Canaan's shore;
There're millions yet within her arm,
And room for millions more.
Now let me praise the great Reformed.
And magnify her name;
For all the kindness she has shown,
Since from the South I came.
She did not turn away from me
But bade me go in peace,
And kindly asked me to accept
A place among the least.
Dear Saviour, bless the great Reformed…

Despite Islay's apparent respect and affection for Dr. See and Dr. Hartranft, pastor of Second Reformed Church in New Brunswick and a professor at the New Brunswick Theological Seminary, the Reformed Church, like other denominations, had divided opinions on how to approach issues of slavery, abolition, and missionary outreach to African Americans. The result was a lack of official commitment. It was not until 1902 that the Reformed Church made a formal commitment to ministry among African Americans.[95] There had been one African American man ordained before Islay. That was the Reverend Dr. W.I. Johnson.

Dr. William I. Johnson

Dr. Johnson was born in New York City in 1844. He graduated from Lincoln University in 1869 and was ordained the next year, 1870, in New York, by the Classis (a Classis is like a diocese, synod, stake, or district) of New York. Claims that he graduated from the New Brunswick Theological Seminary seem unfounded. There were two known references to him graduating from a report by the Board of Domestic Missions made in 1898 and one to the General Synod in 1902. However, his name does not appear in any lists of graduates from the seminary.[96] His obituary did not reference his graduation from the seminary either.[97] In fact, if one follows the timeline, it was highly unlikely that Dr. Johnson could have been at the seminary long enough to graduate. He graduated from Lincoln University in 1869; was ordained the following year, 1870; was an evangelist in North Carolina from 1869 to 1874; was pastor of a church in Somerville, New Jersey, from 1874 to 1875; and was pastor and missionary in Orangeburg, South Carolina, from 1876 until he died in 1913.[98]

A New Endeavor

Even though the Reformed Church might not have had as good a record for its stance on slavery or its ministry to the freedmen as some other denominations, Islay somehow found favor with Dr. Hartranft and Dr. See from the seminary, as well as Professor Atherton at Rutgers College. Not only did these three men go to considerable lengths to help Islay attend Howard University, but they also helped him find funding to attend the seminary. However, he had the same problem as when he was at Howard—how to pay for his other expenses.

Realizing his poetry could help him earn money, Islay turned to it again when he arrived in New Brunswick. He had a scholarship for his tuition. Professor Atherton at Rutgers College had reached out to colleagues and subsequently learned that a man in Yonkers, New York, had left monies to be used specifically to help educate young "colored" men.[99] With that news, Islay was able to officially apply to the seminary, but he still needed money for basic living needs. This time, he penned a series of what he called sacred hymns: *Walden's Sacred Hymns, with a Sketch of his Life.*

The city of New Brunswick took notice right from the beginning. The announcement of the publication of this volume appeared in the *Daily Times* in May 1877:

"Walden's Sacred Poems," to which is added a sketch of the author's life, has just been published. Walden was at one time a slave, but is now a student at the Theological Seminary in this city. From the sale of his books he hopes to

realize a sufficient sum to enable him to pursue his studies until it may be deemed wise for him to enter upon the labors of the ministry among his own race.[100]

A few days later, another notice appeared:

Mr. Islay Walden, the colored student who has been pursuing his studies at the Theological Seminary in this city with the view of entering the ministry of the Reformed Church, is about to visit various places in this state to sell a little book containing his own compositions. His objective is to accumulate enough money to carry on his studies, and as he is eminently deserving, we commend him to the favorable consideration of all on whom he may call.[101]

Publication notices also appeared in North Carolina, in the *North State*,[102] published in Greensboro, North Carolina, and *The Torchlight*,[103] published in Oxford, Granville County, North Carolina. Both notices appeared in August 1878.

Figure 18 John Bergen

Vision Challenges

There was one more hurdle to overcome before the fall term began. Seminary students were required to study Greek and Hebrew. Neither Islay nor John Bergen, the one other student of color, who was also visually impaired, would be able to tackle these subjects. One of the biggest obstacles was the need to learn completely different alphabets for both languages. This was too great a hurdle for either man. They both petitioned to be excused from this requirement. In May 1877, the *Daily Times* reported the outcome:

Messrs. John Bergen and Islay Walden, two colored students from the Theological Seminary were recommended to the General Synod for a dispensation from the course of studies, omitting Hebrew and Greek. One of the candidates, Mr. Bergen is entirely blind and the other, Mr. Walden, is defective. Notwithstanding these deprivations both passed their examinations very creditably. They are to be sent to the South to labor among their brethren there.[104]

The Student Mission

Just as he had been in Washington, Islay was concerned about the African American children of New Brunswick. Once again, he established a Sabbath school. He referenced its history in a September 1878 letter to Dr. Demarest, seminary professor and dean. He explained that one reason he was so intensely involved in the school was because he could not preach at area churches.[105]

As we[106] have no colored churches it is hardly natural to take my turn in preaching on the Sabbath which is a great advantage to those engaged but my work is more arduous than all of theirs as during the past eleven months I have established what is called the students' mission which consists of 60 odd scholars most of which were gathered from the streets, some of which were so poor and destitute that we were not only compelled to fix them up but in many cases I had to buy soap that the peculiar scavengers might be removed. Some two thirds of these were drunkards' children.

Lice and alcoholism. Clearly, Islay had his work cut out for him.

Figure 19 David Demarest

55

Figure 20 First page of handwritten letter to Dr. Demarest,
New Brunswick Theological Seminary.
Courtesy of the Digital Library, Reformed Church in America Archives.

With these conditions, Islay realized there was more needed than just a school for children. There were bigger family issues that needed to be addressed. He understood that children from dysfunctional homes were unable to concentrate on their schoolwork and therefore were less likely to succeed. True to form, Islay created a program. He explained it to Professor Demarest:

With this point in view and the fact that the colored people here have no social nor intellectual advantages so I soon found that the Sabbath school is not enough. Instead of preaching Temperance to these inveterate drunkards I have organized the boys and girls into Temperance societies and sent them forth into every household carrying the idea of temperance. Some parents have entirely reformed.[107]

What a thoroughly innovative approach, using the children to transform their parents! He did not have total success, but clearly, he had an impact.

Figure 21 Senator Samuel C. Pomeroy.
Original Photo by Matthew Brady, Library of Congress

Temperance was not a new concern of Islay's. Islay had expressed his admiration for Senator Pomeroy, a Kansas senator and Howard University trustee who was a strong supporter of both temperance and prohibition. Islay penned a poem, "To Hon. Senator Pomeroy," saying, "These lines were written in honor of the above gentleman, to whom the temperance cause is so much indebted."[108] Of temperance itself, he said:

> *Stretch forth thy loving gentle hand*
> *And raise thy banner to the sky,*
> *Go, save the drunkards of the land,*
> *When others shall have passed them by. ...*
> *Yes, bid the drunkards come to thee,*
> *And save them from the dreadful fall....*[109]

That poem was "composed during the Congressional Temperance Meeting held at Howard University, at which Dr. Chickering presided, and Senator Pomeroy, and others made speeches."[110] This may have been about the time that Senator Pomeroy introduced legislation to the Forty-Second Congress for strict prohibition in the District of Columbia.[111]

Islay's devotion to temperance may have had its origins, at least in part, in a personal experience. That experience was traumatic enough that it was the subject of the second poem he ever composed and the first poem that appears after his introductory poem in his *Miscellaneous Poems*. It is titled "The Danger."[112] According to C.C. Harper, Islay was attacked by a "drunken man" and thereafter sought by a mob, from which he hid in the woods, in fear for his life.[113]

> *Now here I lie upon the ground,*
> *I wonder if I shall be found,*
> *There's nothing but this little pine*
> *By which in safety to recline....*
> *I hear the crew, now passing by,*
> *And wonder if they'll me descry;*
> *For I can hear them loud proclaim,*
> *While swearing vengeance on my name....*
> *I hear their guns and pistols crack,*
> *As though they were returning back....*

For now they pass and do not see,
And surely I shall soon be free,
So, let me rise upon my feet;
It may be that I can retreat.

What Harper did not say was whether the drunken man was a white man whom Islay may have bested to get away, leading to the angry mob pursuing him.

Temperance was not the only social problem Islay attempted to attack on behalf of his students' families:

There is another evil we are trying to remedy, when there is a sickness or death among this people they are nearly all compelled to solicit aid. Now this is the remedy[:] to organize a benevolent society making it beneficial at once instead of delaying six or eight months as most societies do. We are to have no initiation fee but twenty five cents a month tuition in case of sickness. Each member is taxed 5 cents a week and 50 cents at the death of a member. Any member fallen sick who is in the rear he receives 1 cent less from each member for each month that he is behind and such receives 10 cents less from each member for the number of months in the rear. At the end of five months such receive nothing. This is simple and can be done if there are two in the society but the more the merrier.[114]

Islay had the examples of such fraternal organizations as Prince Hall Masons, Oddfellows, and other smaller benevolent societies that African Americans and white Americans had organized.

Islay was not just focused on negative problems to be solved. He also wanted to augment the educational experiences of his students with the musical arts.

There was but one colored girl in this city able to play an organ four months ago. We have a musical class consisting of seven or eight under Miss Lizzie Tenbroek. She is also giving vocal instructions. The class is doing finely. Mr. Colyn had a singing school of some twenty scholars during last winter.[115]

Islay's successes and community support were evident from the very beginning of his creation of the Students' Mission in the many notices that appeared in the *Daily Times*.

In December 1877, notices appeared endorsing his work and asking people to consider contributing to this worthy cause.

The work done by Mr. Islay Walden in this city among the colored people meets the approval of the Christian public. His aim is to improve the social conditions of those of his own race as far as possible. He gathers children into his mission school. Helps to clothe them and, where necessary relieves their physical wants.[116]

The article went on to quote from a notice that had appeared a few days before explaining Islay's intent to start the Students' Mission, wherein Dr. S.M. Woodbridge noted,

He is commended to our citizens for aid in a work that all must feel to be important....Those who desire to assist Mr. Walden in his good work can send contributions to Dr. S.M. Woodbridge, Mrs. William Reilley or to Mrs. J.C. Elmendorf.[117]

Just a few days later, on December 31, another article appeared in the *Daily Times*. The opening sentence clearly implies that New Brunswick had become quite familiar with Islay: "Mr. Islay Walden, the colored student, requests us to publish the following..." The article went on to speak of a recent successful event:

The supper given by contributions of the many friends of the Student's Mission was a complete success in every respect. The children, their parents and many others had supper in common. And after all had been served there seemed to be more provision than when we began, insomuch that bundles were sent to every family of our children and to many others of the poor and needy. Such a supper has never been given before to the colored children of this city. And what is most strange of all is that in the many contributions there was not found a stick of candy. This may be called one step in advance.[118]

Not a stick of candy? There would not be many events involving children today where there would be no candy. He called it an advance. Children today would think they were being deprived. Islay went on to express his appreciation to his many advocates:

Therefore, we express our thanks to the papers of this city whose editors have proved our advocates and also the many responding friends who stand ready to assist us at any time. A deep sense of gratitude toward the Christian Association is felt by scholars and teachers for the use of their rooms for Sunday school purposes.[119]

He ended his thanks to the people of New Brunswick with a quote from the Gospel of Matthew, "Inasmuch as ye did it unto the least of these, ye did it unto me."[120]

Beginning the following year, the school (called the Students' Mission Sabbath-school) and its activities were the subject of a series of articles and advertisements in New Brunswick's *Daily Times*. On December 4, 1878, the *Daily Times* noted that the school had celebrated its first anniversary at the YMCA the previous Sunday. Not only parents and family were in attendance but also members of the First and Second Reformed Churches. The program was described as including prayer, scripture readings, and musical offerings. Monies were also raised in support of the mission for which Walden had "worked laboriously."[121]

On December 21, a small article advertised an upcoming "Panorama and Concert" to be presented on New Year's evening in Saenger Hall at the Seminary. This time the proceeds would go to "the clothing and shoeing of the poor colored children under the care of the mission."[122] The January 4, 1879 edition reported on the concert in an article called "Shoes for the Poor."[123] The event was hailed as a financial success, notwithstanding the theft of four dollars, for which Walden offered a reward for the arrest of the perpetrator. Also noted in the article were "the young ladies who labored to make this and other entertainments of the mission successful,"[124] including an "E.

Farmer," and "P. Farmer," no doubt Eleanora/Elinora Farmer, who would become Islay's second wife, and her sister, Phoebie Farmer, who would follow Elinora to North Carolina and marry Harris Dunson from the Randolph County community.[125]

Leaving New Jersey

Islay had graduated from seminary, was ordained, and now was heading back, back to Lassiter Mills in Randolph County—back to the community he had left ten years earlier, back to his sister, his friends, even his old master, he mused, the one who had first called him a poet.[126] Islay didn't harbor any ill will toward his former enslaver Jesse Smitherman. In a way, he had congenial relations with him and his family. He even had a special bond with one of the daughters, Nancy Jane. In 1872, while away at Howard, he wrote "Miss Nancy Jane" both a letter and a poem.[127] In his introduction to the letter and poem in *Miscellaneous Poems*, he stated, "This letter was written to a little child living in North Carolina, that I used to tend and pet. The first word she spoke was my name."[128] After telling Nancy Jane that he was making good progress with his studies, he added, "I have followed the precepts of your father and mother and for this reason I have run the road of wisdom without getting discouraged."[129] He went on to say that as a Christian he planned to do all he could as a student, as a politician, and as a citizen. He ended the letter with a poem written for her:[130]

> *Miss Nancy Jane, I long to see*
> *Those golden charms of thine,…*

Ultimately, Islay was a man of faith deeply concerned about the spiritual well-being of all he knew. Thus, he continued his poem by asking her,

> *My little friend, I'd like to ask,*
> *Art thou a child of God?*

And do you walk the narrow path
That saints and angels trod?
It is a straight and shining road,
And leads through wisdom's ways,
And if you'd be a child of God,
Oh, start in early days!

He continued his poem by indicating they might never see each other again,

Now, if we never meet again
About the old home place,
Then may we meet in heaven above,
Around God's throne of grace....[131]

Islay concluded by asking her to send his greetings to all his friends and her family. By the time Islay returned to Randolph County, Nancy Jane, or "Nannie" as she was called, was married to Aaron W. Capel and had moved to Richmond County.[132] There is no information on whether Islay ever saw or talked with Nancy Jane again.

Islay may have had a reasonably cordial relationship with his former enslaver's family, but he was clear about the evils of slavery and his sense of relief and gratitude that neither he, nor any person, was enslaved any longer. In his "Address to Dixie," he exults,[133]

And Hallelujahs I am singing,
To see my race from bonds are springing,...
So now farewell to plough and hoeing,
For I to Yankee town am going;
No longer will I drive this wagon,
Nor under slavery's chains be swagging,
But Dixie, oh, the land of cotton,
Let slavery die and be forgotten;...

Islay's faith, however, led him to be optimistic about the future:

> *The races yet will come together,*
> *In ties of love that none can sever.*[134]

Alas, we are still waiting for "[t]he races yet [to] come together, [i]n ties of love that none can sever."

The Journey South

Islay sailed for Virginia just a few days after graduation and ordination, arriving on July 11. The men on the docks in Norfolk and Portsmouth who greeted him were almost all men of color, he wrote back to the *Daily Times* in New Brunswick. His report appeared on July 23 and a month later in the *Goldsboro (NC) Messenger* on August 28, 1879. They were hardworking men, he explained, who had basically good relations with their white co-workers.[135] He explained that he would continue to North Carolina by rail.[136]

Islay was headed to Goldsboro, in Wayne County, but the train went through some smaller communities first, and Islay decided to explore them. He stopped in Mount Olive, North Carolina, today the home of the University of Mount Olive, a small Christian university. He commented, "At all the stations along the railroads, white and colored men seemed to be laboring together as brothers, each trying to earn something to support himself and family."[137] In Mount Olive, he noted, "Many a young man owns his horse and buggy, and nearly all the families own their homes and farms."[138]

From Mount Olive, Islay stopped in Dudley. There he "found the moral standard of this people far superior to any place I was ever at."[139] Dudley, he observed, had an AMA-affiliated school and an educational standard "beyond that of New Brunswick."[140] High praise!

Here I find men owning their own saw and shingle mills, all worshipping under their own "vine and fig tree." Colored men own about this place from one to five or six hundred acres of land.[141]

However, he also witnessed substantial prejudice by the "lower class of the whites toward the colored people," although "those who were wealthy before the war are kindly disposed to them."[142]

Islay finally reached Goldsboro on July 19. He was pleasantly surprised, reflecting that when he left North Carolina he thought it would not be a good place to return (although by all reports he always intended to return), but surprisingly, he found it to be a "fine missionary field."[143] He described Goldsboro as a city of about four thousand people, half of whom were people of color. He noted that four rail lines already passed through the city and two more were planned, all supporting the "great cotton market of Eastern North Carolina."[144] It was also the "centre of the colored population." There was even an asylum for people of color that had been established there.[145] Three churches addressed the spiritual needs of the people of color' one Baptist and two Methodist.

Islay was clearly pleased that there were eight hundred children of color in various schools in Goldsboro: 300 attending common schools; the remainder being taught in Sunday schools, stating he felt "at home" there. His own achievements and reputation prompted community leaders to ask him to stay and establish a high school.[146] The Presbyterian minister sent letters on his behalf to local newspapers introducing him and his work. In addition, the elders of the Presbyterian Church sent letters to Dr. Strieby of the AMA asking for Islay to be assigned to a mission there in Goldsboro. Islay seemed especially impressed because that particular minister had previously enslaved a large number of people but was now "highly honored by the colored people and beloved by all who know him."[147] Other ministers from Baptist, Methodist, and Episcopal Churches also signed the letter. The Methodist minister said it was "a field very much in need of cultivation," while the Episcopal minister called it "an excellent field."[148] Islay ended his report saying that "other citizens of high standing will write to Dr. Strieby giving their testimony of the importance of the field."[149] Based on these comments, it seems that Islay hoped to stay in Goldsboro. This may have been the offer that he reportedly turned down before returning to Randolph County, rather than an offer in New Jersey. For reasons unknown, Islay did not stay in Goldsboro but returned to Randolph County. Perhaps Dr. Strieby reminded him that when signing with the AMA, he had agreed to return to his community in Randolph County and bring them the advantages of educational opportunity that Goldsboro already enjoyed. In any event, by November 1879, he had returned to Randolph County, when an AMA field superintendent, Reverend Dr. Joseph Roy, visited him.[150] Islay was living with his sister and her family in an area in the Uwharrie Mountains, in southwestern Randolph County called by the locals "Hill Town."[151]

Back in the Uwharries

At last, Islay was home, in the same Uwharrie Mountain community where his sister, Sarah, wife of Emsley Hill, lived. The community was called Hill Town, named for the many Hill family members and their families who lived there. He wasted no time establishing a Congregational church and "common school," as AMA one- or two-teacher schools were called.

In November 1879, Dr. Joseph Roy,[152] a field secretary with the American Missionary Association, wrote, "The Field Superintendent assisted [Islay Walden] in organizing a Congregational Church of thirty members."[153] Roy stated that a man in Hill Town offered "three acres of land and timber in the tree for all the lumber needed for a church school-house, and that man was an ex-slave."[154] It is not clear to whom he was referring, since the Hill family had been free since before 1850.

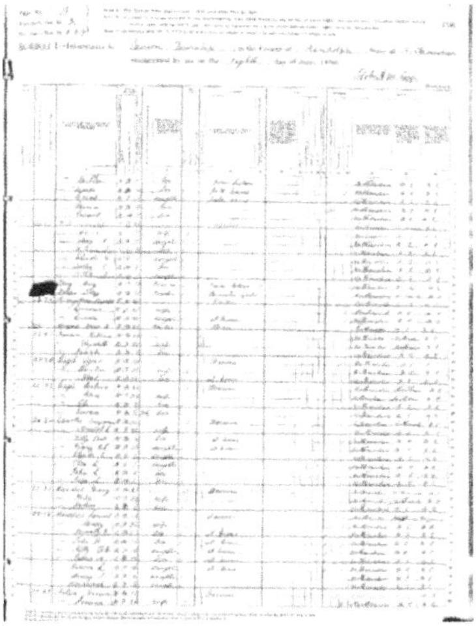

Figure 22 Islay Walden, 1880 Census, Brower Township, Randolph County, North Carolina

**Figure 23 Rev. Joseph E. Roy, Field Secretary of
the American Missionary Association**

Dr. Roy noted that he met with three committees, one from Hill Town, one from what would become Salem Church, in Concord Township, about eight miles away, and one from Troy, in neighboring Montgomery County, where the AMA was in the process of establishing Peabody Academy. At this point they did not have an ordained minister for each location, so they created a circuit:

So we organized a circuit for Brother Walden, one Sabbath at Troy and the other at Salem Church and Hill Town, with one sermon at each place. The Quakers promise a school at Salem. A public school will serve Hill Town for the present, and a competent teacher must be secured for the Academy.[155]

Islay's church community in Hill Town grew quickly and soon needed a property large enough to support a church, schoolhouse, and cemetery. In 1880, just one year after returning home to the Uwharrie Mountain community where he was once enslaved, Islay, as agent for the AMA, purchased six acres from a nearby white family, Addison and Cornelia Lassiter, on which the church was built.[156]

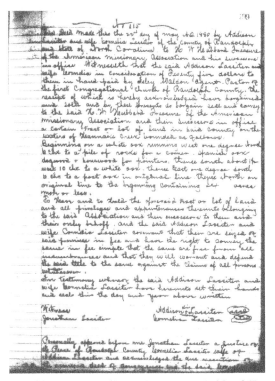

Figure 24 Addison & Cornelia Lassiter to H W Hubbard, Treasurer, American Missionary Association, paid by Islay Walden, Agent & Pastor, First Congregational Church of Randolph County.

Dr. Roy wrote about the building of the church in a letter to the Reverend John Mason Ferris, secretary of the Reformed Church's Board of Foreign Missions:

And so upon a beautifully rounded crest stands the church, a frame 29x45, with fifteen feet posts, finely "weather-boarded," floored and roofed, with a door, window, and nothing more. Without plastering, or ceiling, or pews, or paint, or pulpit, or stove or bell, we yesterday dedicated this House of the Lord. With great joyfulness the multitude gathered into their own sanctuary, saying, "The Lord hath done great things for us, whereof we are glad," while the same was said of them by the many white citizens who came out only to be amazed at what they saw. The sermon was upon the building and the dedicating of the Temple by the ex-captives....At the dedication the people christened their sanctuary the "Promised Land Church," but Canaan was for all the world.[157]

Years later, Kate Lassiter Jones, a church member and descendant of some of the first congregants, wrote:

Men and women gathered from every direction to plan for the building. A two-wheeled ox cart hauled six huge rocks for the foundation. Logs, lumber, and service were given. The weather boarding for the 60'x30' building was finished by hand, mostly by our late Uncle Julius Hill.[158]

With that, First Congregational Church of Randolph County became Promised Land Church and School.

Figure 25 Promised Land/ old Strieby Church, Union Township, Randolph County, North Carolina, replaced by the current church building in 1972

Figure 26 Strieby Church, School, and Cemetery Site Map — Tax Parcel 29596.

The Church members at Hill Town quickly became involved in the wider life of the Congregational Church and the American Missionary Association. A report of the 1880 Conference held at Dudley, North Carolina, noted that representatives traveled 130 miles to attend. In describing the progress of the church at Hill Town, it said, "A gracious revival and a meeting-house under way are the fruits of the first six months of the life of this church."[159]

The following year, in 1881, the report again mentioned Islay and others from the congregation:

Rev. Islay Walden and his delegate, Deacon Potter, together with three others, came fifty miles in a one-horse wagon to attend the Conference. One of the party, Mrs. Hill, now a widow, has had twelve children, forty grand-children and twelve great-grand-children. She had never seen the (train) cars nor heard a railroad whistle till she came to the Conference....The sermon Friday night was by Rev. Islay Walden; text, the first Psalm.[160]

Most certainly the "Mrs. Hill" referenced here was Priscilla Hill, affectionately called "Granny Prissy," the matriarch of the Hill family, for whom Hill Town was named.[161] "Deacon Potter" could have been Thomas Potter, her son-in-law, married to her daughter Mary Jane Hill,[162] or possibly Thomas's brother, Ira Potter, married to daughter Charity Hill.[163]

Figure 27 Priscilla (Mahockley) Hill, "Granny Prissy."

One to Love

The year 1881 brought other new, more personal changes in Islay's life. He married a woman he met while studying in New Jersey.[164] Elinora/Eleanora Wilhelmina Farmer was the daughter of John and Catherine Farmer.[165] Despite her northern urban background, she became an important part of Islay's work in Hill Town and Randolph County, becoming a teacher and principal of the school at Hill Town.[166]

Figure 28 Marriage Record of (Alfred) Islay Walden and Eleanora/Elinora W. Farmer, 1881, New Brunswick, New Jersey.

Islay had longed for a wife and companion for many years. Going back to his time at Howard University and his first volume of poems, he wrote about his desire for someone to share his life in "One to Love":

> Oh, where's the maid that I can love,
> With love which I have never told?
> Where is the one that I would like
> To comfort me when I am old?
> Do I not see before my face,
> A mate prepared for every one?
> Then sure there's one prepared for me,
> Nor need I trudge the road alone.[167]

Islay believed it was important to have a mate as seen in his advice to a Howard University graduating class, possibly that of 1872:

> ...When entering on the field of life,
> Each graduate should have a wife,
> One who will guide his feet aright,
> And ever be his heart's delight....[168]

Several poems and letters indicate that Islay had actively pursued several young women, possibly including the Miss Johnson for whom he advocated to Howard University.[169] She may have been the "Miss N.J." to whom he wrote on August 19, 1872, just four days before he wrote to Miss Crane, at Howard University, to plead for a Miss Johnson to be accepted as a student.[170]

> Miss N. J.**, I my pen have taken,...
> Because thou hast my heart and mind....
> On thee I look with much compassion,...
> How would'st thou like to be with me?
> O! wilt thou try to come to college,
> Where wisdom teacher's do impart,...
> I might tell thee my heart is willing'

That I should be thy guide through life,
But while I am not worth a shilling,
Why should I seek thee for a wife?…
My friend I know that I'm a student
Preparing for some distant land;
Pray tell me if it would be prudent,
Were I to ask thee for thy hand?
For I can see stamped in thy features
What never living man has seen,
That thou wouldst make a handsome creature,
And also me a loving queen.

Who was Miss N.J.? If we assume that Miss N J. and Miss Johnson were one and the same person, we could make a guess that the "N" stands for Nancy. Since Islay was writing to her in August 1872, she might be in the 1870 census. Based on a letter Islay wrote to Dr. Hartraft in October1872, Islay was staying with Dr. Hartraft in August 1872. However, there was no Nancy Johnson of appropriate age identified in the 1870 or 1880 censuses. Miss N.J. might have been the Nancy Johnson in the 1860 census for New Brunswick. That Nancy Johnson was about eighteen years of age, living with a white family, the MacDonalds, working as a domestic servant.[171] As noted earlier, there is no indication that Miss N.J. ever did attend Howard, nor is there any information that the relationship between Islay and Miss N.J. ever became more serious or continued. In the end it did not matter, because Islay married a different New Jersey girl, Elinora Farmer.

1883

By 1883, Promised Land Church and the Hill Town community were growing, a testament to the great success that Islay and his wife, Elinora, were having both with the church and the school. Islay's influence in the community was evident when, on March 2, 1883, the North Carolina General Assembly passed

an Act to prohibit the sale of spirituous liquors within one (1) mile of the Promise Land Academy in New Hope Township,[172] *among other places in Randolph County.*[173]

This was consistent with Islay's efforts to combat alcoholism among the families at the Student Mission in New Brunswick, as well as his support of the Temperance Society in Washington, D.C. However, Islay had even bigger plans for the Hill Town community and Promised Land Church and School.

A New Post Office

Islay was tired of the long ride to the Lassiter's Mill Post Office, over two miles away in neighboring New Hope Township. Besides, the Hill Town community was growing. Why shouldn't it have its own post office? So, in 1883, he petitioned the government for a post office. It was granted. That was not all that was granted. Islay asked not only for the new post office to serve Hill Town, but also that the community have a new name — Strieby, in honor of the Reverend Dr. Michael E. Strieby, corresponding secretary of the American Missionary Association.

The Reverend Dr. Michael E. Strieby

The Reverend Dr. Michael E. Strieby was born in Ohio in 1815. While a student at Oberlin, he became heavily involved with the antislavery movement and intensely committed to helping those seeking freedom. Though a beloved Congregational minister for over ten years, he was called to be the corresponding secretary of the American Missionary Association. In that capacity, he was known for "encouraging despondent teachers, gathering about him a great mass of Negroes, just freed from bondage, seeking to inspire them with purposes of self-control and self-direction."[174] Dr. Strieby died on March 16, 1899.[175]

M. E. Strieby

Figure 29 The Rev. Michael E. Strieby, D. D.

From Hill Town to Strieby

One can assume that Dr. Strieby had in some way both inspired and encouraged Islay. Unfortunately, no direct correspondence between them has been located to date. Nevertheless, Islay's admiration for Dr. Strieby inspired him enough to transform the community of Hill

Town into Strieby, with Islay as the first postmaster. In February 1884, the *American Missionary* wrote:

Rev. Islay Walden's school and church whose post-office was formerly that of Lassiter's Mill, have now secured a new post route and their own post-office, called by the government Strieby, and served by the pastor as postmaster.[176]

Strieby Post Office would last until 1940, when other dynamics dictated reallocation of postal services.

Figure 30 US Postmasters -Strieby

Illness and Death

The excitement generated around this event came to an abrupt halt when Islay died unexpectedly from acute bronchitis (more likely pneumonia) on February 2, 1884, at the age of forty. The *American Missionary* wrote,

He rallied the people, developed a village with school-house and church, secured a post-office and became postmaster. Here he labored four years, blessed with revivals, and was honored by the people, black and white. His wife an educated and judicious missionary teacher was of great assistance to him in all his work.[177]

The *People's Advocate*, a Washington, D.C. newspaper for African Americans, published a notice in April of Islay's death. The paper said that Islay was a *"born missionary"* (emphasis added). It also reminded readers that ten years previously, when he was a student in Washington, he had established "a very successful mission school at the Columbia Law Building."[178]

Despite his short life, by all measures, Islay had been successful. He had gone from being enslaved, controlled by others, to being a free man, community leader, postmaster, and ordained minister whom others followed. He went from being illiterate to a university and seminary graduate, published poet and educator. He went from being another man's property to owning property. At his death, his probate indicated that he owned three tracts of land totaling 194 acres and had an "equitable interest" in a fourth tract of land.[179]

Islay was buried in Strieby Church Cemetery. Originally, the spot was marked only by a large field stone; today there is a modest stone marker.[180] The church and school that he began, as well as the post office he established, would now be left to others to care for and cultivate. Although his ministry was cut short, he had accomplished much, worthy of the biblical praise: "Well done, thou good and faithful servant....[E]nter thou into the joy of thy lord."[181]

Figure 31 Headstone of the Rev. Islay Walden, Strieby Congregational Church Cemetery, Asheboro, Randolph County, North Carolina.

The Legacy

Despite Islay's death at an early age, he did leave a legacy. He is best known for his legacy of poetry. However, that would not be his only legacy, nor would it be the legacy he most hoped for and worked toward. The legacies he sought were those of education and spiritual development. Nevertheless, all of his life's work would have a significant and lasting influence on his community in Randolph County.

The Legacy of Poetry

Certainly, there was a legacy of poetry. Islay was one of the first freedmen to have his poetry published. As such, his work has been analyzed and evaluated by various academics who specialize in nineteenth-century African American poetry.

Joan Sherman, professor emerita of English literature at Rutgers University, included Islay and his poems in all three of her books on nineteenth-century African American poetry. In her 1992 *Anthology*, referencing *Miscellaneous Poems*, she wrote:

His frankness, affectionate regard for people, naïve waggish humor, and natural joy in living give special charm to verses on love and such homespun occasions as eating at school, ice skating, and needing a winter overcoat.[182]

On the other hand, Sherman was not a fan of *Walden's Sacred Hymns*, reportedly calling it "uninspired and repetitious."[183] Ben Friedlander noted that after acquiring an education, Walden no longer expressed his poetry in a "folk" manner. Friedlander explained that unlike Langston Hughes, Islay "didn't live at a time when he might have been both sophisticated and folk."[184] Dickson

Bruce wrote of Walden in his book *Black American Writing from the Nadir: The Evolution of a Literary Tradition 1877–1915*:

At the center of Walden's poetry was a deep devotionalism. The poems focused on an emotional relationship between the believer and God and on the hope for a heavenly union.[185]

Echoing this sentiment. Simmons-Henry, Henry, and Speas, in *The Heritage of Blacks in North Carolina*, noted that "the Christianity that Walden preached, he exemplified in his life."[186]

Blyden Jackson in "Black Victorian Writers of North Carolina" said that Islay was "the first Black North Carolina writer who could be called Victorian."[187] Bruce expanded on this in the *Oxford Companion to African American Literature*, saying that Walden and other Reconstruction-era/Victorian-era African American writers "created paeans to nature, love, and a sentimental piety. They broke with other Victorians only in persistently linking their writing to protesting prejudice and discrimination."[188] On the other hand, Gene Jarrett wrote in his introduction to *African American Literature beyond Race: An Alternative Reader* that if one agreed with the critique that there were poets who emphasized form over content, a neoclassical hallmark, then Islay would be considered a "neoclassical" poet.[189] Jarrett quotes Joan Sherman, saying that writers such as Islay "'show a decided bias for neoclassical decorum, heightened poetic diction, and technical virtuosity.'"[190] Later in *Deans and Truants: Race and Realism in African American Literature*, Jarrett notes that Islay and his African American contemporaries "produced enough poems to suggest that their literary tradition was not an anomaly, but a racial fixture.[191]

Perhaps the most important indication that Islay's poetry was not an insignificant contribution to nineteenth-century poetry can be seen in an article that appeared in the *Pittsburgh Courier*, then a relatively new publication, but one that went on to be considered a giant among African American newspapers. On September 2, 1911, it ran an article written by N. Barnett Dodson about the founding of a new historical research society dedicated to preserving African American history by Arthur A. Schomberg and John E. Bruce, aka Bruce Grit, the same Bruce Grit who sang for Islay's Sabbath school presentation at Howard University.

The new organization was called the Negro Society for Historical Research and was established for "the purpose of gathering information from books and through correspondence of historical value to the Negro race."[192] The article stated that the society had already acquired 150 titles: "A few of the more important ones are here given:…'Poems of Islay Walden,' blind poet of North Carolina, 1875."[193] This article also appeared in the *Lexington (KY) Standard* on October 21, 1911,[194] and *Franklin's Paper the Statesman*, also on October 21, 1911.[195] Islay's poetry and other titles and photographs would eventually become part of the Schomburg Center for Research in Black Culture, in New York City.

There is some information that Islay wrote another volume of poems around 1875, called *The Ritual of the Golden Circle.*[196] Because no copies are known to exist, the exact nature of these poems is not known. It is possible that he was writing in response to activities of the Knights of the Golden Circle (KGC). The KGC was organized to promote disunion, slaveholding, and the southern way of life. Members planned to set up a headquarters in Mexico with a view to "Americanization" and "Southernization" of Mexico. Membership qualifications for the Third Degree, or political degree, stated:[197]

Candidate must be familiar with the work of the two former Degrees. Must have been born in 58 (A slave State) or if a 56 (A free State) must be a citizen, 60 (A Protestant), and 61 (A slaveholder). A candidate who was born in 58 (A slave State) need not be 61 (A slaveholder) provided he can give 62 (Evidences of character as a Southern man).

One could assume that Islay criticized the KGC in his poem, but without any copies available, just what he said is speculation.

Nevertheless, even without this poem, Islay's poetry provides a lasting contribution to the legacy of nineteenth-century African American thought.

Both of Islay's collections have been reprinted in recent years and made available to the public once again. His poems are considered important examples of nineteenth-century African American poetry. They are included in a variety of anthologies as well as poetry websites. However, that was not the legacy for which he longed.

An Educational Legacy

Islay's desire for a legacy of education and spirituality did not die with him in 1884. Others who shared his dream and vision picked up the mantle. Primary among them was his widow, Elinora Farmer Walden, who continued as the principal teacher and postmistress.[198] "Mrs. Elinora Walden continues the school work of her husband, greatly confided in by the people."[199] The ministerial work was assumed by the Reverend Zachariah Simmons, who was then pastor at Salem Congregational Church in nearby Concord Township.

Figure 32 Henry Ruffin Walden

Another person to step in was Henry Ruffin Walden, a cousin of Islay's. In 1888, as Henry was about to enter his final year as a student in the Normal program at Hampton Institute, he married Elinora Walden, Islay's widow.[200] After graduating in 1889, he returned to Strieby to become a teacher there. An entry for his name in a Hampton Institute publication stated: "Teaching with his wife (whom he married before entering the Senior class) the American Missionary School at Strieby, NC."[201] The following year, 1890, the biennial report of the superintendent of public instruction noted that "Strieby Normal School" was one of only two schools for "colored" children in Randolph County; the other was in Asheboro, the county seat. Elinora was listed as the principal, and there were thirty-four students in attendance.[202]

Sadly, Elinora died in early 1892. Her obituary appeared in the March 1892 issue of the *American Missionary*:

At the time of her death, she held the position of Principal of Garfield Academy, at Strieby, was postmistress, and was working very hard in a series of meetings which were being held and in which several of her pupils had found the Saviour.[203]

Figure 33 Eleanora W. Walden Tombstone, Strieby Church Cemetery, Asheboro, North Carolina

Elinora was also buried in Strieby Cemetery next to Islay. Henry would stay on for about ten years, eventually remarrying[204] and pursuing his own ministry elsewhere in North Carolina. Strieby School itself continued into the 1920s, when it was absorbed by the public school system and merged with two other small rural common schools, Salem School (also begun by Islay) and Red House School.

Islay's wish for a common school in the area that his niece Catherine could have attended had come true. However, by the time he returned to Randolph County, Catherine had married and moved away, settling eventually in Ohio.[205] Nevertheless, Islay had brought education to the African American communities of southwestern Randolph County. He planted the seeds for the love of education that would bear fruit for generations to come.[206] He would be gratified to know that over the years, Strieby students would attain an unusually superior level of achievement for a small, rural, African American common school, evidenced, for example, by nearly every young man from the community being able to sign their World War I draft cards in cursive.[207] In addition, Strieby graduates would go forth as teachers in their own right, teaching at Strieby, in the combined school that succeeded Strieby, at Peabody Academy, and elsewhere in North Carolina and beyond.[208]

A Spiritual Legacy

Although the school is long gone, Strieby Church continued to hold regular services into the early years of the twenty-first century. In recent years, services and Bible study have been led by various family members, including the Reverend Winston Lassiter; his wife, the Reverend Tanya (Le'Gette) Lassiter; the Reverend Eric Ratliff Sr.; Elder Elbert Lassiter Jr.; and Trustee, Jerry Laughlin. Elbert and Jerry grew up attending Strieby Church.

Ultimately, younger family members sought educational and job opportunities elsewhere in North Carolina and around the country. The changing demographics eventually drained Strieby of its community and congregation. With a dwindling community, the post office closed. Strieby community was no more.

Nevertheless, Strieby continued to hold an important place in the hearts and minds of descendants. The annual homecoming services, on the fourth Sunday in August, have continued to be held in the new church building, built in 1972. In addition, Strieby descendants continue to bury their loved ones in the cemetery next to their ancestors. They have kept alive Islay's dream.

Figure 34 Strieby Congregational UCC Church, Asheboro, North Carolina

A Cultural Legacy

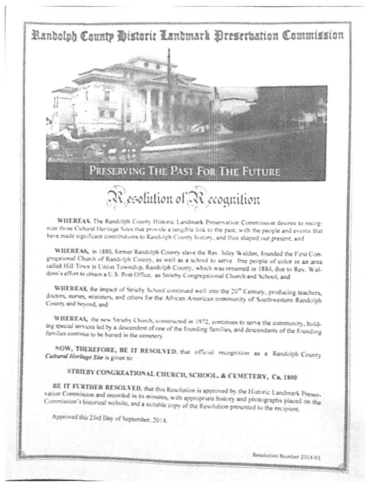

**Figure 35 Randolph County Historic Landmark Preservation
Commision "Resolution of Recognition" approving Strieby Church,
School & Cemetery as a Cultural Heritage Site, 23 September 2014.**

On September 23, 2014, the cultural impact of Strieby's church and school was recognized by the Randolph County Historic Landmark Preservation Commission (HLPC).[209] By gathering and presenting to the commission the history of the church and school that Islay started, at their monthly meeting, the community has been able to preserve and lift up the history of Islay's church and school for the world to see. The commission agreed that the Strieby Church, School and Cemetery property was an important Cultural Heritage Site in Randolph County. A slide presentation of the history as well as site pictures were uploaded to the HLPC website and copies preserved in their files. A sign at Strieby Church provides visible testimony for all who venture down Strieby Church Road that Islay's vision for the community of Hill Town came to fruition and that Strieby Church and Cemetery continue to be an important part of the historical and cultural heritage of Randolph County. In 2020, Islay's vision, Strieby Church, celebrated its 140th anniversary.

Afterword

Islay Walden is primarily remembered for his poetry. However, Islay's use of poetry was not just a means of personal expression but a vehicle to pursue his true passions, education and ministry. The fruits of those passions are at the forefront of his remembrance in Randolph County, North Carolina, his home. It is there that his Promised Land Church and its common school, both renamed *Strieby*, guided generations of African Americans in the Strieby community and surrounding areas for over one hundred years. It could be said that the life which he dedicated "to the cause of education and humanity," succeeded in bearing fruit for generations.

If you enjoyed reading about Islay Walden's life, ministry, and poetry, please share a review at Amazon, Barnes & Noble, Goodreads, or On-Line Book Club.

———————

or leave me a comment on the website at,
Personal Prologue: Family Roots and Personal Branches,
https://margoleewilliamsbooks.com/islay-walden.

Also, be sure to follow me on Facebook (@personalprologue),
Instagram (@margoleewilliams),
Twitter (@MargoLW1228), and LinkedIn (@Margo L., Williams).

Appendix

Ancestry of Islay Walden

Islay's paternal ancestry has been the source of speculation for years.[210] At the end of the war, Islay, formerly enslaved by Jesse Smitherman, chose Walden as his surname. Most have said that William D. Walden, a free man of color from southeastern Randolph County, was his father. However, Islay said otherwise.

As noted elsewhere herein, he said his father's name was Branson Walden on his marriage license to Amelia Harriss, in 1867, while in Raleigh, North Carolina. In his death notice in the *American Missionary*, they said his father's name was Branson Garner, reflecting Islay's enslaver's name when he was born and suggesting that his father was someone associated with the same enslaver. In addition, Islay told the reporter from the *New York Evening Star* that his father had run away to the west on false papers. This confirms that his father had been enslaved, not free. The one fact that seems to be consistent with the suggestion that he was related to William D. Walden seems to be his choice of Walden as his surname and, according to him, his father's surname.

Islay's association with a Walden family is strengthened by Henry Ruffin Walden, his mother, Julia Ritter Walden, and his sister, Tima Walden McLeod, and her family leaving neighboring Moore County to move to Strieby after Islay died, leaving behind his widow, Elinora. There seems to be no compelling reason to do so other than potential familial ties. What were those ties? Was there also a tie to William D. Walden's family?

Interestingly, William D. Walden, Henry Ruffin Walden, and Islay Walden all had shared given names in their respective families.

William D. Walden had brothers named Anderson and Branson (Stephen Branson); Henry Ruffin Walden's father and Julia Ritter Walden's husband was also Anderson. They also had a son in their family, brother to Henry Ruffin and Tima, named General Branson. One additional coincidence was that Anderson, free born and from Randolph County, had a brother, John Chavis Walden, who had moved to the Raleigh area of Wake County. By 1870, Anderson himself had moved to Raleigh and was staying with John Chavis's son, next door. It was not a stretch to believe that Islay, when passing through Raleigh in 1867, stayed with the family or visited, at least. Again, we ask, what was the relationship of the two Anderson Waldens, one who headed a free family, the other who headed an enslaved family?

In the Census

The first **Anderson Walden** (herein, **Anderson-1**) was a free man of color born about 1800. He was the oldest of the four sons of **William Walden** and **Levina (Goins?) Walden**.[211] They lived in the Southern Division of Randolph County in 1840[212] and 1850.[213] In 1860, the census divided the county into Eastern and Western Divisions, rather than Northern and Southern. Anderson-1 was living in the Eastern Division of Randolph County, in the Foust Mills P.O. community.[214] In 1870, Anderson-1 was living in Wake County, in the home of his nephew, **Haywood Walden**,[215] son of Anderson-1's younger brother, **John Chavis Walden**, and **Martha Evans Walden**.[216]

The second **Anderson Walden** (herein, **Anderson-2**) was born enslaved about 1817, most likely in Moore County. There is no evidence he ever lived in Randolph County, but without knowing who all his enslavers were, there is no way to say definitively. His wife, **Julia Ritter Walden**, and children[217] were also from Moore County. Anderson-2 Walden never appeared in any census records because he was known to be enslaved prior to 1865. He did not appear in the 1870 census, the first census to be taken after the end of slavery, because he died in 1869, as reported in the U.S. Federal Mortality Schedules.[218]

Family Members

Anderson-1 married **Sally Walden**, on November 30, 1830, in Randolph County.[219] Her parents have not been identified to date. Anderson-1 and Sally had the following known children: *Thomas, Delana, Mosley, Brantley,* and *John W.* Sally was apparently dead by 1850, when all names of household members were recorded on the census. In 1850, the household of Anderson-1 included all his known children, but Sally was missing.[220] In 1860, his household included "Bartley" [*sic*] and John.[221] In 1870, as noted previously, Anderson-1 was living in Wake County, with his nephew, **Haywood Walden**, son of his brother, **John Chavis Walden**.[222]

Anderson-2 did not live long enough to be included with his family in any census records, having died in 1869.[223] He was known to be the husband of **Julia Ritter Walden** of Moore County, who was also enslaved. Anderson-2 and Julia Ritter Walden had twelve known children: *Bethania, Elizabeth, John W., Anderson Jr., James A., General Branson* (remember that Islay Walden said his father's name was Branson), *Tima, Rebecca, Rhoda, Julia Ann, Margaret,* and *Henry Ruffin.* In 1870, the first census after the end of slavery, Julia was living with eight of her children: Anderson, James, General B., Tima, Rebecca, Rhoda, Julia Ann, Margaret, and Henry Ruffin.[224] **Bethania** was married to **Jerry Ritter,**[225] and **Elizabeth** was married to **Samuel Ritter.**[226] **John W.** might be the John Walden with **Mary Walden** (his first wife was said to be **Mary Caveness**[227]) and a small boy, **McKay,** on the 1870 census,[228] but in 1874, he married **Margaret Ann Myrick** in Moore County.[229]

Naming Patterns

As noted, **Anderson-2** and **Julia** had a son named **General Branson Walden**. This child may have been named for a possible sibling of Anderson's, **Branson Garner/Walden**, the father of **Islay Walden**[230] who escaped west on falsified papers.[231] The potential sibling relationship between Anderson-2 and Branson is supported by the fact that **Julia**, her youngest son, **Henry Ruffin Walden**, and her daughter **Tima** and her husband, **Jerry McLeod**, left Moore County and moved to Strieby after the death of Islay. This was most likely to help Islay's widow, **Elinora W. Walden**, with the school, since Henry was also studying to be a teacher at Hampton University, then called Hampton Institute.[232] Henry married Elinora in 1888.[233] Julia remained in the Strieby area, where she died in 1907, and was buried in Strieby Church Cemetery.[234] Julia and Anderson-2's daughter **Tima Walden McLeod** and her husband, **Jerry McLeod**, who also moved to Strieby, had a daughter Eugenia, who also became a teacher and who would eventually marry the Reverend Zachariah Simmons. Reverend Simmons became Strieby's minister. **Tima** and

Jerry McLeod were also buried in Strieby Cemetery.[235] It seems likely that Julia, Henry, and Tima moved to Strieby after Islay's death because he was family. There seems little else to explain it.

What about William D. Walden?

As noted, researchers have speculated for years that **Islay Walden** was a son of **William D. Walden**, Anderson-1's brother. However, we know from research that Islay himself reported that his father's name was **Branson**. He reported further that his father had been enslaved, but he had escaped from his enslavers by using falsified identity papers. Was it possible that the family oral history that Islay's father was a free man may have been conflated over the generations? Could it have been Islay's grandfather, Branson's father, who was the free man of color? Again, all evidence is strictly circumstantial.

If it is assumed that **Anderson-2** and **Branson** were siblings, the fact that the two men have the same names as **Anderson-1** and his brother, **Stanford** B., whose middle name is believed to have been "Branson," points to a potential family relationship. It could mean that one of the free Walden brothers had a relationship with an enslaved woman who was the mother of the presumed enslaved siblings, prior to a legal marriage to a free woman, but which brother?

Anderson-1 was old enough to be the father of the presumed siblings, **Anderson-2**, **Branson**, and a probable sister, **Tima**, who married **Brantley Strickland**. Anderson-1 was born about 1800,[236] making him about seventeen or eighteen when **Anderson-2** was born. No age is known for **Branson**, but **Tima** was born around 1820,[237] making Anderson-1 about twenty when she was born. Tima was also found to be living in Brower's Township in 1870,[238] where Anderson-1's brother **William D. Walden** was also living[239] and where he and his brothers had grown up. Branson was likely born about the same time period. Those facts combined with the fact that Anderson-1 did not marry until 1830 and that the oldest of the presumed enslaved siblings, Anderson-2, had the same name as Anderson-1, potentially making them senior and unior, all point to Anderson-1 being the likely candidate. What about the other brothers?

John Chavis Walden was born about 1807.[240] He was too young, being only ten years old in 1817 and only thirteen in 1820. (Remember that Anderson-1 and the John Chavis family were all living in Wake County when Islay stopped in Raleigh on his way to Washington, D.C.) Neither **William D.**, born about 1817,[241] nor **Stanford B.**, born about 1828,[242] were old enough. Thus, the most plausible candidate for the father of the three potential siblings, Anderson-2, Branson, and Tima, is Anderson-1. However, there is no evidence known to exist that can corroborate or refute this theory. Therefore, it is merely a working hypothesis.

Genealogical Summary

Anderson Walden (William1), called here **Anderson-1,** was born about 1800, the son of **William Walden** and his wife, **Levina (Goins?) Walden**. They lived in the southeastern part of Randolph County, North Carolina.[243] He died sometime between 1870 and 1880, most likely in Wake County, where he was last found living in 1870.[244] He married **Sally Walden** on September 30, 1830, in Randolph County.[245] She died before 1850. They had the following children: *Thomas*, *Delana*, *Mosley*, *Brantley*, and *John W. Walden*.[246] He may also have been the father of *Anderson-2*, *Branson*, and *Tima Walden* by an unknown enslaved woman.

Anderson Walden (father unknown), called here **Anderson-2**, was born about 1817.[247] He may have been the son of Anderson-1 Walden and an unknown enslaved woman of Randolph County. He was presumed to live most of his adult life in Moore County, where he died in October 1869.[248] He was married to **Julia Ritter**, date unknown. They were both enslaved.[249] Julia was born about 1822 in Chatham County.[250] She died on January 15, 1907, in Strieby,

Randolph County, where she is buried in Strieby Church Cemetery.[251] Anderson-2 and Julia Ritter had the following children: *Bethania, Elizabeth, John W., Anderson Jr., James A., General Branson, Tima (possibly named for the older Tima Walden Strickland), Rebecca, Rhoda, Julia Ann, Margaret,* and *Henry Ruffin*.[252]

If one assumes that these two Andersons were father and son and that Anderson-1 was also the father of Branson, father of Islay Walden, it would be logical for Anderson-2's widow, Julia Ritter Walden (who would therefore be Islay's aunt by marriage) and her children Henry Ruffin and Tima (who would be Islay's first cousins) to move to Strieby after Islay's death to help his widow, Elinora.

About the Author

Figure 36 Margo Lee Williams.
Photo by Marvin T. Jones

Margo Lee Williams is an award-winning genealogy and history author. A former editor of the *Journal of the Afro-American Historical and Genealogical Society*, she is particularly interested in community and family histories of people of color in the Southeast, especially those in North Carolina and Virginia, who often had mixed-race origins.

Williams has researched and written extensively on her Lassiter family of Randolph County, North Carolina. Her first book, *Miles Lassiter (circa 1777–1850) An Early African American Quaker from Lassiter Mill, Randolph County, North Carolina: My Research Journey to Home* (Backintyme Publishing, 2011), relates the personal and research journeys that led to the discovery of her fourth great-grandfather Miles Lassiter. Her second book, *From Hill Town to Strieby: Education and the American Missionary Association in the Uwharrie "Back Country" of Randolph County, North Carolina*

(Backintyme Publishing, 2016), is a social history that follows the development of the school and church founded in 1880 by the Reverend Islay Walden. Her research led to the church and former school property being named a Randolph County Cultural Heritage Site in 2014. Both of Williams's books have won genealogy and history book awards.

Williams is a graduate of Marquette University. She has her master's degree in sociology from Hunter College and her master's in religious education from the Catholic University of America. She worked for over twenty years at various churches in the suburban Washington, D.C. area and another eight years as a National Service Officer with Vietnam Veterans of America. She is currently the project historian for a grant study of the Historical Black Families of Sandy Spring, Montgomery County, Maryland.

Sources

Addison & Cornelia Lassiter to H.W. Hubbard. (1880). Randolph County, North Carolina Deed Book 42:199.

American Missionary Association. "Anniversary Reports: North Carolina." *American Missionary* 35, no. 7 (1881).

———. "Items from the Field." *American Missionary* 38, no. 4 (1884)

———. "The Field: North Carolina." *American Missionary* 38 (1884).

———. "North Carolina Conference." *Annual Report of the American Missionary Association* 34 (1880): 72.

———. "Obituary: Mrs. Henry R. Walden." *American Missionary* 46, no. 3 (1892): 91.

———. "Our Spring Associations." *American Missionary* 38, no. 6 (June 1884):164–65.

———. "Report." *American Missionary* 49, no. 5 (1895).

———. "Rev. Michael E. Strieby, D.D." *American Missionary* 53, no. 1 (1899): 1.

———. "Revival Work—Significant Facts." *American Missionary* 38, no. 4 (1884).

Barker, Louisa J. "Testimony of a Northern Woman." *Freedmen & Southern Society Project*, January 1864. http://www.freedmen.umd.edu/Barker.html.

Beardslee, J.W., III. "The Reformed Church in America and African Americans," *Western Seminary Journal*, 1992, 108. https://repository.westernsem.edu

Brooklyn Daily Eagle. "Personal: Walden." August 8, 1873.

Bruce, Dickson D. *Black American Writing from the Nadir: The Evolution of a Literary Tradition 1877–1915*. Baton Rouge: Louisiana State University Press, 1992.

― ― ―. "Reconstruction Era." In *The Concise Oxford Companion to African American Literature*, edited by W.L., Andrews, R. F. Smith and T. Harris, 451–53. New York & Oxford: Oxford University Press, 1997.

Bruggink, D.J., and K.N. Baker. *By Grace Alone: Stories of the Reformed Church in America*. Grand Rapids, MI: Wm. B. Erdmanns Publishing, 2004.

Brumm, J.H., ed. "The Experience of Black People in the Reformed Church in America." In *Equipping the Saints: The Synod of New York, 1800–2000*, 71–85. Grand Rapids, MI: Wm. B. Ermanns Publishing, 2000.

Chase, W.C., ed. "Flotsam and Jetsam," *Washington Bee*, September 17, 1898, 4.

Christian Intelligencer. "Correspondence: Rev. Joseph Roy Letter to Ferris." November 11, 1880.

Daily Times (New Brunswick, NJ). "Anniversary of Students' Mission." December 4, 1878.

― ― ―. "City Matters." March 24, 1879.

― ― ―. "City Matters." June 30, 1879.

― ― ―. "City Matters: Mr. Islay Walden." May 25, 1877.

― ― ―. "College and Seminary Notes." May 16, 1879.

― ― ―. "Indorsed." December 26, 1877.

― ― ―. "Indorsed." December 28, 1877.

― ― ―. "Islay Walden's Ordination." July 2, 1879.

― ― ―. "Meeting of Classis." May 24, 1877.

― ― ―. "Ordained." June 28, 1879.

― ― ―. "Ordinations." June 25, 1879.

― ― ―. "Panorama and Concert." December 21, 1878.

― ― ―. "Shoes for the Poor." January 3–4, 1879.

— — —. "Student's Mission." December 31, 1877.

— — —. "Students' Mission." March 29, 1879.

— — —. "Walden's Sacred Poems." May 19, 1877.

— — —. "Where There's a Will, There's a Way: Panorama and Concert." December 28, 1878, 3.

Davis, W.A., ed. "State News: Islay Walden." *The Torchlight*, August 6, 1878.

DeBoer, C. M. "Blacks and the American Missionary Association." United Church of Christ. http://www.ucc.org/about-us_hidden-histories_blacks-and-the-american.

Dodson, N.B. "Select Society for Research." *Pittsburgh Courier*, September 2, 1911.

— — —. "Select Society for Research." *Lexington Standard*, October 21. 1911.

— — —. "Select Society for Research," *Franklin's Paper The Statesman*, October 21, 1911.

Estate of Islay Walden. North Carolina, Estate Files, 1663–1979, index and images. Randolph County, 1884.

Evening Post (New York, NY). "An Interesting Ordination." July 2, 1879.

Evening Star. "The Fifteenth Amendment." April 2, 1870.

— — —. "Local News: Howard University — Normal Class." June 16, 1876.

— — —. "Remarks by Mr. Sumner." April 2, 1870.

Find a Grave. "Strieby Congregational United Church of Christ Cemetery. Julia Walden, 15 Jan 1907 (Asheboro, Randolph County, North Carolina)." https://www.findagrave.com.

— — —. "Strieby United Church of Christ Cemetery. Tima S. Waldon McLeod, died 4 May 1908; Jerry McLeod, died 26 Apr 1908." https://www.findagrave.com.

Foreman, Carolyn T. "Marshalltown, Creek Nation." *Chronicles of Oklahoma* 32, no. 1 (1954): 52–57.

Friedlander, B. "The Birth of Poetry." American Poetry in the Age of Whitman and Dickenson. https://ampoarchive.wordpress.com/2009/10/08/birth-of-poetry/#comments

Garner, H. Lacy. *From Slavery to Strieby: Rev Alfred Islay Walden, 1843–1884.* Lulu Publishing, 2011.

General Council. "North Carolina: Lassiter's Mill." In *The Year Book of the Congregational Christian Churches of the United States*, 176. Boston: Alfred Mudge & Son, 1884.

Goodhue County. "Personal and Literary: Islay Walden." July 24, 1873.

Grant, M. "Strieby: Never Heard of It." *Asheboro Magazine* 1, no. 11 (2011): 56–58.

Hammond, L., and C.L. Cranford. *Farmer, Yesterday and Today: Families, Individuals, Churches, and Schools.* Lexington, NC: Wooten Printing, 1982.

Hampton Institute. "Henry Walden." In *Twenty-Two Year's Work of the Hampton Normal and Agricultural Institute at Hampton, Virginia*, 290. Hampton, VA: Normal School Press, 1893. GooglePlay eBook.

Hollyday, J. *On the Heels of Freedom: The American Missionary Association's Bold Campaign to Educate Minds, Open Hearts, and Heal the Soul of a Divided Nation.* New York: Crossroad Publishing Company, 2005.

"Howard University Normal Department Class of 1876: Islay Walden Deceased." In *Alumni Catalogue of Howard University with List of Incorporators, Trustees, and Other Employees, 1867–1896*, 44. Washington, D.C.: Union Alumni Association, 1896. https://archive.org/stream/alumnicatalogue00howa/alumnicatalogue00howa_djvu.txt.

Irons, S. "John Edward Bruce (1856–1924)." Black Past, July 18, 2007. https://www.blackpast.org/african-american-history/bruce-john-edward-1856-1924.

Jackson, Blyden. "Black Victorian Writers of North Carolina." *Victorians Institute Journal* 12 (1984): 55.

— — —. "Islay Walden." In *Dictionary of North Carolina Biography*, edited by William S. Powell, 108–9. Chapel Hill: University of North Carolina Press, 2009.

— — —. "Islay Walden." NCpedia. http://NCpedia.org/biography/walden-islay.

Jarrett, G.A. "Introduction." *African American Literature Beyond Race: An Alternative Reader*. New York: New York University Press, 2006.

— — —. *Deans and Truants: Race and Realism in African American Literature*. Philadelphia: University of Pennsylvania Press, 2007.

Jones, Kate L. "History of the Strieby Congregational United Church of Christ." In *Souvenir Journal for the Dedication of the New Church Building: Strieby Congregational United Church of Christ*, 1–2. Strieby, NC: Strieby Congregational United Church of Christ, 1972.

"KGC." CNY Artifact Recovery. https://cnyartifactrecovery.wordpress.com/kgc.

Kilcup, K.L., and A. Sorby. *Over the River and through the Wood: An Anthology of Nineteenth Century Children's Poetry*. Baltimore: Johns Hopkins University Press, 2013.

King James Bible (KJV) Online. https://www.kingjamesbibleonline.org.

Lancaster Examiner. "Republican State Convention." March 18, 1868.

Larsen, K., ed. *The Cambridge Companion to Nineteenth-Century American Poetry*. New York: Cambridge University Press, 2012.

Lewis, J.D. "North Carolina Education — Randolph County." Carolana. www.carolana.com/NC/Education/nc_education_randolph_county.html

Logan, Rayford W. "Education of Youth in the Liberal Arts and Sciences." In *Howard University: The First Hundred Years, 1867–1967*, 35–38. New York: New York University Press, 1969.

Martin, Stella, and Frederick Douglass, eds. "The Fifteenth Amendment." *New Age*, February 10, 1870.

Mount Zion African American Episcopal Church. "About Us: Our History." https://www.mountzioname.org/about_us.

National Council. "Vital Statistics." In *The Congregational Yearbook, 1885*, 37. Boston: Congregational Publishing Society, 1885.

National Republican. "Howard University." June 15, 1876.

National Temperance Society. *A Memorial Volume of the Centennial Temperance Conference Held in Philadelphia, PA., September 1885*. Philadelphia: National Temperance Society and Publication House, 1885.

New Brunswick Theological Seminary. "Alfred Islay Walden." http://www.nbts.edu/newsite/estory.cfm?storynum=154.

New Brunswick Theological Seminary Anti-Racism Transformation Team. "Slavery, Justice and New Brunswick Theological Seminary." February 25, 2016. http://www.nbts.edu/slavery-justice-and-new-brunswick-theological-seminary.

New Jersey, Marriages, 1678–1985 [Database online]. "Alfred I. Walden and Elenor W. Farmer, 18 May 1888." FamilySearch. Retrieved from https://familysearch.org/pal:/MM9.1.1/FZPL-QY7.

North Carolina, Marriage Index, 1741–2004 [Database online]. "H.R. Walden and Eleanor W Walden, December 13, 1888." Ancestry. Retrieved from www.ancestry.com.

North Carolina, Marriage Records, 1741–2011 [Database online]. "Aaron W. Capel and Nancy Jane Smitherman, December 31, 1878, Randolph County." Ancestry. Retrieved from www.ancestry.com.

— — —. "Alfred I. Walden and Amelia Frances Harriss, October 17, 1867, Wake County." Ancestry. Retrieved from www.ancestry.com.

— — —. "Anderson Walden and Sally Walden, married: September 30, 1830, Randolph County." Ancestry. Retrieved from www.ancestry.com.

— — —. "Catherine Hill and Shubal Ingram, March 15, 1877, Randolph County." Ancestry. Retrieved from www.ancestry.com.

— — —. "Harris Dunson and Phoebe Farmer, April 3, 1890, Randolph County." Ancestry. Retrieved from www.ancestry.com.

— — —. "Haywood Walden and Lucrettie Walden, Married: September 13, 1893, Wake County." Ancestry. Retrieved from www.ancestry.com.

— — —. "Henry Walden and Theodosia Hargrove, 13 September 1898, New Hanover County." Ancestry. Retrieved from www.ancestry.com.

— — —. "Ira Potter and Charity Hill, 10 October 1865, Randolph County." Ancestry. Retrieved from www.ancestry.com.

— — —. "Nancy Jane Smitherman and Aaron W. Capel, December 31, 1878, Randolph County." Ancestry. Retrieved from www.ancestry.com.

— — —. "Thomas J. Potter and Mary Jane Hill, December 29, 1867, Randolph County." Ancestry. Retrieved from www.ancestry.com.

North Carolina, Wills and Probate Records, 1665–1998 [Database online]. "Estate of James Gardner: Sale of Slaves, Court of Common Pleas and Quarter Sessions, August 1844 Term." Ancestry. www.ancestry.com.

— — —. "William Walden, Probate Date: 1842." Ancestry. www.ancestry.com.

North State. "Islay Walden." August 1, 1878.

The (Harrisburg, PA) Patriot. "Personal: Islay Walden." July 18, 1873.

Penkava, L., ed. "Strieby Church Named Cultural Heritage Site." *Randolph Guide*, October 7, 2014. http://www.randolphguide.com/news/local_news/article_ab 8b5180-4e36-11e4-9cd2-8b547d0b5025.html.

Pennsylvania State University. "Penn State Presidents: George W. Atherton." Penn State University Libraries. https://libraries.psu.edu/about/collections/penn-state-university-park-campus-history-collection/george-w-atherton.

People's Advocate. "Personal: Rev. Islay Walden." April 5, 1884.

Poetry Foundation. "Alfred Islay Walden, 1847–1884." http://www.poetryfoundation.org/bio/alfred-islay-walden

Randolph County, North Carolina Historic Landmark Preservation Commission. "Meeting Minutes, September 23, 2014." http://www.co.randolph.nc.us/hlpc/minutes/hlpc_minutes_1 40923.pdf.

— — —. "Randolph High School Cultural Heritage Site." http://www.co.randolph.NorthCarolina.us/hlpc/RandolphHi ghSchool.htm.

— — —. "Strieby Church Cultural Heritage Site." http://www.co.randolph.NorthCarolina.us/hlpc/StriebyChurc h.htm.

Redwood Gazette. "Personal and Literary: Islay Walden." July 31, 1873.

Reformed Church in America. "Minutes of General Synod: Directory and Financial Reports. Appendix 1." In *The Acts and Proceedings of the Seventy-First General Synod*, 689. New York: Board of Publication of the Reformed Church in America, 1877. https://books.google.com

The Representative. "Personal and Literary: Islay Walden." August 1, 1873.

Richardson, J.M., and M.D. Jones. *Education for Liberation: The American Missionary Association and African Americans, 1890 to the*

Civil Rights Movement. Tuscaloosa: University of Alabama Press, 2009.

Rockford Journal. "Personal and Literary: Islay Walden." July 26, 1873.

Roy, Joseph E. "The Freedmen," *The American Missionary*. 3, no. 11 (1879): 334–35.

Sandifer, Alex, and Berry Dishong Renfer. "Schools for Freed People." NCpedia. https://www.ncpedia.org/education/freed-peoples.

Saxon, W. "The New York Post Has a Long History." *New York Times*, November 20, 1976.

Sherman, Joan. "Alfred Islay Walden." In *African-American Poetry of the Nineteenth Century: An Anthology*, 221; 222–35. Champaign: University of Illinois Press, 1992.

— — —. "Alfred Islay Walden." In *Invisible Poets; Afro-Americans of the Nineteenth Century*, 104–11. Champaign: University of Illinois Press, 1974.

Simmons-Henry, L., P. Henry and C. Speas. *The Heritage of Blacks in North Carolina*. Raleigh: North Carolina African American Heritage Foundation, 1990.

The Standard. "Condensed News: Islay Walden." July 31, 1873.

The Thirtieth Annual Report of the American Missionary Association. New York: American Missionary Association [hereafter AMA], 1876.

Tomar, D.A. "George Atherton: Patron Saint of Penn State." *The Quad*. https://thebestschools.org/magazine/penn-state-george-atherton.

Trenton State Gazette. "Local Items: Islay Walden." July 31, 1871.

U.S. School Catalogs, 1765–1935 [Database online]. "Howard University: Alson D. Bemo, Marshalltown, Indian Territory, Class B, Model School, 1872." Ancestry. ancestry.com.

– – –. "Clara Saunders, Howard University Normal Department, Model School, Class D: 1872." Ancestry. ancestry.com.

– – –. "Howard University: Islay Walden, Ashborough, North Carolina, Class D, Model School, 1871." Ancestry. ancestry.com.

– – –. "Howard University: Margaret M. Wright, Washington, D.C., Miner School, 1872." Ancestry. ancestry.com.

– – –. "Howard University: Mary W. Warrick, Class A, Model School, 1872." Ancestry. ancestry.com.

– – –. "Howard University: Thomas V.R. Gibbs, Tallahassee, Florida, Class B, Model School, 1872." Ancestry. ancestry.com.

"Walden, Alfred Islay." North Carolina Literary Map. http://library.uncg.edu/dp/nclitmap/details.aspx?typ=auth&id=1754.

Walden, Henry Ruffin. *Family Record of Anderson and Julia Walden: From 1822–1907*. Rockingham, NC: Henry Ruffin Walden, 1909.

– – –. "Missionary Work at Strieby, N.C." *American Missionary* 45, no. 3 (1891): 166–69.

– – –. "Teaching the Young." *American Missionary* 47, no. 10 (1893): 318–19.

Walden, Islay. "Introduction." *Walden's Miscellaneous Poems: Which the Author Desires to Dedicate to the Cause of Education and Humanity*. Hong Kong: Forgotten Books Classic Reprint, 2012. Reprint.

– – –. "Letter to Prof. David Demarest from Islay Walden (ca. 1845–1884) of the NBTS Class of 1879, One of the First Two African American Graduates of the School." *Reformed Church in America: Following Christ in Mission*, n.d. http://www.nbts.edu/wp-content/uploads/2016/02/Alfred_Islay_Walden_Letter.pdf.

– – –. *Walden's Miscellaneous Poems*. Washington, D.C.: self-published, 1873. Google Books.

— — — . *Walden's Sacred Poems with a Sketch of His Life*. New Brunswick, NJ: Terhune & Van Anglen's Press, 1877.

— — — . "What an Educated Colored Man Thinks of Goldsboro." *Goldsboro Messenger*, August 28, 1879.

Walker, J.D. "Strieby Church, School, and Cemetery Become Latest Randolph County Cultural Heritage Sites." *Courier-Tribune*, September 23, 2014.

Washington Daily Chronicle. "Official: Lists of Letters Remaining in the Washington City Post Office August 26 – Men's List." August 20, 1870.

Williams, Margo Lee. "The Autograph Book of Lela Virginia Farnell Williams." *Journal of the African American Historical and Genealogical Society* 17, no. 1 (1998). The original autograph was donated by the author to the Meek Eaton Black Archives at Florida A&M University in 2014.

— — — . "1891, the Year of the African American Postmistress — Elinora W. Walden," Personal Prologue. https://margoleewilliamsbooks.com.

— — — . *From Hill Town to Strieby: Education and the American Missionary Association in the Uwharrie "Back Country" of Randolph County, North Carolina*. Crofton, KY: Backintyme Publishing, 2016.

— — — . *The History of Strieby Congregational Church and School, Union Township, Randolph County, North Carolina: Cultural Heritage Site Application*, 2014. http://www.co.randolph.nc.us/hlpc/downloads/Strieby_Church_and_School_History.pdf

— — — . "Once upon a Time in Hill Town." *Courier-Tribune* (Asheville, NC), February 2015.

— — — . "Will Anderson Walden Please Stand? Distinguishing between Two Men of the Same Name." Personal Prologue: Family Roots and Personal Branches, February 23, 2019. margoleewilliamsbooks.com.

Wilmington Daily Commercial. "Notices." September 9–14, 1870.

The World. "City and Suburban Items: Islay Walden." July 12, 1873.

Census Records

All census records retrieved from ancestry.com

U.S. Federal Census Mortality Schedules, 1850–1885. "Anderson Walden, Blacksmith, married; died: Oct 1869, Ritter's, Moore County, NC."

1840

1840 U.S. Federal Census. Census Place: South Division, Randolph County, North Carolina; Anderson Walden, head; and John C. Walden, head. NARA Roll: M704-369; Page: 57; Family History Library Film: 0018097.

— — —. Census Place: South Division, Randolph County, North Carolina; William Walden, head. NARA Roll M704-369; Page 56; Family History Library Film: 0018097.

1850

1850 U.S. Federal Census. Census Place: North Brunswick, Middlesex, New Jersey; Jane Hougland, head, age 60; Joseph, age 24; Jane, age 15. NARA Roll: M432-455; Page: 250A; Image: 509.

— — —. Census Place: Southern Division, Randolph County, North Carolina; Anderson Walden, head. NARA Roll: M432-641; Page: 88B; Image: 182.

— — —. Census Place: Southern Division, Randolph County, North Carolina; Stanford Walden, head, born 1828. NARA Roll: M432-641; Page: 88B; Image: 182.

— — —. Census Place: Southern Division, Randolph County, North Carolina; William D. Walden, head, b. 1817. NARA Roll: M432-641; Page: 88B; Image: 182.

— — —. Census Place: Western Division, Wake County, North Carolina; John Walden, head, age: 43. NARA Roll: M432-647; Page: 198B; Image: 400.

1860

1860 U.S. Federal Census. Census Place: Eastern Division, Randolph County, North Carolina; Anderson Walden, head. NARA Roll: M653-910; Page: 320; Family History Library Film: 803910.

— — —. Census Place: New Brunswick, Middlesex, New Jersey; William McDonald, head; Nancy Johnson, age 16, servant, Page: 362. NARA M653; Family History Library Film: 803700.

1870

1870 U.S. Federal Census. Census Place: Browers Township, Randolph County, North Carolina; Brantley Stricklin, head; Tima Stricklin, wife. NARA Roll: M593-1156; Page: 317B; Family History Library Film: 552655.

— — —. Census Place: Browers Township, Randolph County, North Carolina; William D. Walden, head. Roll: M593-1156; Page: 319A; Image: 87; Family History Library Film: 552655.

— — —. Census Place: Philadelphia, Ward 7, Pennsylvania, William Dunlap, head; Page: 226; NARA microfilm publication M653, Family History Library Film: 805157.

— — —. Census Place: Ritters, Moore County, North Carolina; Jerry Ritter, head; Bethany Ritter. NARA Roll: M593-1149; Page: 577A; Image: 273916; Family History Library Film: 552648.

— — —. Census Place: Ritters, Moore County, North Carolina; Julia Walden, head. NARA Roll: M593-1149; Page: 579A; Family History Library Film: 552648.

— — —. Census Place: Ritters, Moore, North Carolina; Samuel Ritter, head; Elizabeth Ritter/ NARA Roll: M593-1149; Page: 576B; Image: 273903; Family History Library Film: 552648.

— — —. Census Place: Sheffields Township, Moore County, North Carolina; John Walden, head. NARA Roll: M593-1149; Page: 607A; Family History Library Film: 552648.

— — —. Census Place: White Oak, Wake County, North Carolina; Haywood Walden, head; Anderson Walden, birth year about 1803. NARA Roll: M593-1163; Page: 439B; Family History Library Film: 552662.

— — —. Census Place: White Oak, Wake County, North Carolina; John Walden, head. NARA Roll: M593-1163; Page: 439B; Family History Library Film: 552662.

1880

1880 U.S. Federal Census. Census Place: New Brunswick, Middlesex, New Jersey; NARA Roll: 789; Family History Film: 1254789; Page: 79B; Enumeration District: 122; Image: 0586. John V. Farmer, head; Elinore W. Farmer, daughter; Phoebie A. Farmer, daughter.

— — —. Census Place: Union, Randolph, North Carolina; Roll: 978; Family History Film: 1254978; Page: 196C; Enumeration District: 224; Image: 0683. Emsley Hill, head; Islay Walden, boarder.

— — — —. Census Place: Union Township, Randolph County, North Carolina; Priscilla Hill, head. NARA Roll: 978; Family History Film: 1254978; Page: 195B; Enumeration District: 224; Image: 0682." Ancestry. Retrieved from ancestry.com.

1900

1900 U.S. Federal Census. Census Place: Carthage, Moore County, North Carolina; John Walden, head; Margaret Walden, wife; married about: 1874. Page: 8; Enumeration District: 0068; FHL microfilm: 1241207.

Index

Notes

Ordination

[1] "City Matters," *Daily Times*, June 30, 1879.

[2] The 1850 census records a Jane Hoagland, a free woman of color, living in New Brunswick, Middlesex County. The census records her age as sixty, indicating that she would be born about 1790. That would be about the right age to be the Mount Zion foundress. it appears she was most likely widowed with two probable children, Joseph (probably named for her husband) and Jane. Joseph was aged twenty-four, and Jane was fifteen. See 1850 U.S. Federal Census [hereafter USFC].

[3] Mount Zion African American Episcopal Church, "About Us: Our History," mountzioname.org. It should be noted that slavery was ended in New Jersey in 1804, by gradual emancipation,

[4] Psalm 19:14, KJV, https://www.kingjamesbibleonline.org/Psalms-Chapter-19.

[5] The Reformed Church in America derived from the Dutch Reformed Church.

[6] The Reverend William Johnson, who was ordained by the Classis of New York in 1870, has been reported to be a graduate of the seminary; however, this author has not found any contemporaneous citations. All reports of him being a graduate come from the 1890s or later. See Bruggink and Baker, *By Grace Alone*.

[7] "Ordinations," *Daily Times*, June 25, 1879.

[8] Saxon, "New York Post Has a Long History," *New York Times*.

[9] "Interesting Ordination," *Evening Post*, July 2, 1879.

[10] I. Walden, "Letter to Prof. David Demarest."

Looking Back

[11] Pennsylvania State University, "Penn State Presidents: George W. Atherton."

[12] Notices, *Wilmington Daily Commercial*, September 9–11, 1870.

[13] 1870 USFC. For an additional discussion of Islay Walden's ancestry, see the appendix: "Ancestry of Islay Walden."

[14] North Carolina, Marriage Records, 1741–2011, "Alfred I. Walden and Amelia Frances Harriss."

[15] North Carolina, Wills and Probate Records, 1665–1998, "Estate of James Gardner."

[16] C.C. Harper, "Introduction," in *Miscellaneous Poems* (1873), 8, GooglePlay ebook.

[17] "Republican State Convention," *Lancaster Examiner*, March 18, 1868.

[18] I. Walden, "Ode to Mr. Dunlap and Family," *Miscellaneous Poems* (1873), 77.

[19] Ibid.

[20] Ibid.

[21] Ibid., 76.

[22] 1870 USFC.

[23] I. Walden, "Ode to Mr. Dunlap and Family," 76.

[24] Ibid., 78.

[25] I. Walden, "Place Thy Trust in God," *Miscellaneous Poems* (1873), 94.

A Witness to History

[26] Martin and Douglass, "Fifteenth Amendment."

[27] "Fifteenth Amendment," *Evening Star*, April 2, 1870.

[28] I. Walden, "Little Helper," *Miscellaneous Poems* (1873), 29.

[29] U.S. School Catalogs, 1765–1935, "Clara Saunders."

[30] "Remarks by Mr. Sumner," *Evening Star*, April 2, 1870.

[31] I. Walden, "The Nation's Friend," *Miscellaneous Poems* (1873), 25–27.

[32] Ibid., 27.

Seeking and Education

[33] "Notices," *Wilmington Daily Commercial*, September 9–14, 1870.

[34] Harper, "Introduction," 8.

[35] Barker, "Testimony of a Northern Woman."

[36] Harper, "Introduction," 9. It is curious that when mentioning Dr. Nichols and Sarah Nichols in the book *Howard University: The First Hundred Years, 1867–1967*, Rayford Logan claimed the relationship between Dr. Nichols and Sarah was unknown.

[37] I. Walden, "To My Benefactor," *Miscellaneous Poems* (1873), 36.

[38] I. Walden, "To S.S.N.," *Miscellaneous Poems* (1873), 14.

[39] Harper, "Introduction," 9.

[40] Pennsylvania State University, "Penn State Presidents: George W. Atherton."

[41] U.S. School Catalogs, 1765–1935, "Islay Walden."

[42] Logan, "Education of Youth in the Liberal Arts and Sciences," in *Howard University*, 35–38.

[43] I. Walden, "To Professor Atherton," *Miscellaneous Poems* (1873), 70.

44 "Local Items: Islay Walden," *Trenton State Gazette*, July 31, 1871.

45 In 1879, Dr. Hartranft became a professor at Hartford Theological Seminary, in Connecticut, eventually its president.

46 I. Walden, "Letter to Rev. Mr. Hartraught [*sic*]," *Miscellaneous Poems* (1873), 57.

47 I. Walden, "Letter to Miss Crane," *Miscellaneous Poems* (1873), 55–56.

48 I. Walden, "Our May-Day Walk," *Miscellaneous Poems* (1873), 34.

49 I. Walden, "To the Faculty of Howard University," *Miscellaneous Poems* (1873), 52.

Life at Howard

50 "Local News: Howard University — Normal Class," *Evening Star*, June 16, 1876, 5.

51 Ibid.

52 "Condensed News," *The Standard*, July 31, 1873.

53 "Personal," *The Patriot*, July 18, 1873, 2.

54 "Personal and Literary," *Goodhue County*, July 24, 1874.

55 "Personal and Literary," *Redwood Gazette*, July 31, 1873.

56 "Personal and Literary," *Rockford Journal*, July 26, 1873.

57 "City and Suburban Items," *The World*, July 12, 1873.

58 "Personal," *Brooklyn Daily Eagle*, August 8, 1873. Note: Professor A. Barber was Professor Amzi Barber, principal of the Normal Department at Howard University.

59 I. Walden, "Letter to Dr. See," *Miscellaneous Poems* (1873), 42.

60 I. Walden, "Dedicated to the Junior Society," *Miscellaneous Poems* (1873), 88–89.

61 I. Walden, "To Miss W*****," *Miscellaneous Poems* (1873), 74–75.

62 U.S. School Catalogs, 1765–1935, "Margaret M. Wright."

63 I. Walden, "Ode to Gen. O.O. Howard," *Miscellaneous Poems* (1873), 38–39.

64 I. Walden, "Dedicated to a Young Lady," *Miscellaneous Poems* (1873), 59–62.

65 U.S., School Catalogs, 1765–1935, "Alson D. Bemo."

66 Foreman, "Marshalltown, Creek Nation," 52.

67 I. Walden, "Correspondent Solicited," *Miscellaneous Poems* (1873), 91–92.

68 I. Walden, "A Lady Friend," *Miscellaneous Poems* (1873), 47.

69 I. Walden, "Dedicated to M.W.W.," *Miscellaneous Poems* (1873), 37–38.

70 U.S. School Catalogs, 1765–1935, "Mary W. Warrick."

71 I. Walden, "On a Seamstress," *Miscellaneous Poems* (1873), 44.

72 U.S. School Catalogs, 1765–1935, "Victoria Shaw."

The Sabbath School

73 Sandifer and Renfer, "Schools for Freed People."

74 I. Walden, "Call to Sabbath School," *Miscellaneous Poems* (1873), 45.

[75] U.S. School Catalogs, 1765–1935, "Thomas V.R. Gibbs."

[76] Williams, "Autograph Book." The autograph book was donated by the author to the Meek Eaton Black Archives at Florida A&M University in 2014.

[77] Williams, *From Hill Town to Strieby.*

[78] I. Walden, "Prayer for The School," *Miscellaneous Poems* (1873), 18.

[79] W.C. Chase, "Flotsam and Jetsam: Islay Walden," *The Washington Bee,* September 17,1898, 4. Newspapers.com.

[80] S. Irons, "John Edward Bruce (1856-1924)," *Black Past,* July 18, 2007. Blackpast.org

[81] Chase, "Flotsam and Jetsam," September 17, 1898.

[82] NYPL, "Schomburg Center for Research in Black Culture," nypl.org.

[83] Dodson, "Select Society for Research," *Pittsburgh Courier,* September 2,1911.

[84] Dodson, "Select Society for Research," *Lexington Standard,* October 21, 1911.

[85] Dodson, "Select Society for Research," *Franklin's Paper The Statesman,* October 21, 1911.

A Spiritual Calling

[86] I. Walden, "Jesus, My Friend," *Miscellaneous Poems* (1873), 15–16.

[87] I. Walden, "Doubts and Fears," *Miscellaneous Poems* (1873), 15.

[88] I. Walden, "Place Thy Trust in God," *Miscellaneous Poems* (1873), 94–95.

[89] I. Walden, "My Refuge," *Miscellaneous Poems* (1873), 20.

[90] I. Walden, "Place Thy Trust in God," 94–95.

[91] Ibid.

[92] Ibid.

[93] Ibid.

[94] Ibid., 95.

New Brunswick

[95] Bruggink and Baker, *By Grace Alone,* 101–4.

[96] Ibid., 104.

[97] Beardslee, "Reformed Church in America," 108.

[98] Bruggink and Baker, *By Grace Alone,* 104.

[99] "Interesting Ordination," *Evening Post,* July 2, 1879.

[100] "Walden's Sacred Poems," *Daily Times,* May 19, 1877.

[101] "City Matters: Mr. Islay Walden," *Daily Times.* May 25, 1877.

[102] "Islay Walden...," *North State,* August 1, 1878.

[103] Davis, "State News," *The Torchlight,* August 6, 1878.

[104] "City Matters: Mr. Islay Walden," *Daily Times,* May 25, 1877, 3.

The Student Mission

105 I. Walden, "Letter to Prof. David Demarest."
106 Here Islay is referencing the lack of Reformed congregations of color.
107 I. Walden, "Letter to Prof. David Demarest."
108 I. Walden, "To Hon. Senator Pomeroy," *Miscellaneous Poems* (1873), 65.
109 I. Walden, "Temperance," *Miscellaneous Poems* (1873), 19.
110 Ibid., 19.
111 National Temperance Society, *Memorial Volume*, 202.
112 I. Walden, "The Danger," *Miscellaneous Poems* (1873), 13.
113 Harper, "Introduction," 8.
114 I. Walden, "Letter to Prof. David Demarest."
115 Ibid.
116 "Indorsed," *Daily Times*, December 26, 1877, 3.
117 Ibid.
118 "Student's Mission," *Daily Times*, December 31, 1877.
119 Ibid.
120 Ibid.
121 "Anniversary of Students' Mission," *Daily Times*, December 4, 1878.
122 "Panorama and Concert," *Daily Times*, December 21, 1878.
123 "Shoes for the Poor," *Daily Times*, January 3–4, 1879.
124 Ibid.
125 Ibid. See also 1880 USFC.

Leaving New Jersey

126 Harper, "Introduction," 8.
127 Walden, "Letter to Miss Smitherman," *Miscellaneous Poems* (1873), 20–21.
128 Ibid., 20.
129 Ibid., 21.
130 Ibid.
131 I. Walden, "Address to Dixie," *Miscellaneous Poems* (1873), 82.
132 North Carolina, Marriage Records, 1741–2011, "Nancy Jane Smitherman and Aaron W. Capel."
133 I. Walden, "Address to Dixie," 82.
134 Ibid., 83.

The Journey South

135 I. Walden, "What an Educated Colored Man Thinks," *Goldsboro Messenger*, August 28, 1879.
136 Ibid.
137 Ibid.
138 Ibid.

[139] Ibid.
[140] Ibid.
[141] Ibid.
[142] Ibid.
[143] Ibid.
[144] Ibid.
[145] Ibid.
[146] Ibid.
[147] Ibid.
[148] Ibid.
[149] Ibid.
[150] Roy, "Freedmen," 334–35.
[151] 1880 USFC.

Back in the Uwharries

[152] See W.E. Barton, *Joseph Edwin Roy, 1827–1908* (Oak Park, IL: Puritan Press, 1908).
[153] Roy, "Freedmen," 334–35.
[154] Ibid.
[155] Ibid.
[156] Addison and Cornelia Lassiter to H.W. Hubbard, May 22, 1880, Randolph County, North Carolina Deed Book 42:199.
[157] "Correspondence": Roy letter to Ferris, *Christian Intelligencer*, November 11, 1880.
[158] Katherine L. Jones, dedication of Strieby Congregational UCC Church, 1972, 2.
[159] American Missionary Association, "North Carolina Conference," 72.
[160] American Missionary Association, "Anniversary Reports: North Carolina," 211.
[161] 1880 USFC.
[162] North Carolina, Marriage Records, 1741–2011, "Thomas J. Potter and Mary Jane Hill."
[163] North Carolina, Marriage Records, 1741–2011, "Ira Potter and Charity Hill."

One to Love

[164] New Jersey, Marriages, 1678–1985, "Alfred I. Walden and Elenor W. Farmer."
[165] 1880 USFC.
[166] American Missionary Association, "The Field," 45.
[167] I. Walden, "One to Love," *Miscellaneous Poems* (1873), 24.
[168] I. Walden, "To the Graduating Class," *Miscellaneous Poems* (1873), 46.

[169] I. Walden, "Letter to Miss Crane," *Miscellaneous Poems* (1873), 55.
[170] I. Walden, "To Miss N.J.," *Miscellaneous Poems* (1873), 66.
[171] 1860 USFC.

1883

[172] Though physically in Union Township, the postal address for the community, including the church and school, was at the Lassiter's Mills Post Office in neighboring New Hope Township.
[173] Lewis, "North Carolina Education."
[174] American Missionary Association. "Rev. Michael E. Strieby, D.D.," 2.
[175] Ibid.
[176] American Missionary Association, "Items from the Field," 51.
[177] American Missionary Association. "Revival Work," 98.
[178] "Personal: Rev. Islay Walden," *People's Advocate*, April 5, 1884.
[179] Estate of Islay Walden.
[180] National Council, "Vital Statistics."
[181] Matthew 25:21 KJV

The Legacy

[182] Sherman, "Alfred Islay Walden," 221.
[183] Ibid.
[184] Friedlander, "Birth of Poetry."
[185] Bruce, *Black American Writing*, 22–24.
[186] Simmons-Henry, Henry and Speas, *Heritage of Blacks*, 70.
[187] Jackson, "Black Victorian Writers," 55.
[188] Bruce, "Reconstruction Era," 451.
[189] Jarrett, "Introduction," 12.
[190] Ibid.
[191] Jarrett, *Deans and Truants*, 43.
[192] Dodson, "Select Society for Research," *Pittsburgh Courier*, September 2, 1911.
[193] Ibid.
[194] Dodson, "Select Society for Research," *Lexington Standard*, October 21, 1911.
[195] Dodson, "Select Society for Research," *Franklin's Paper The Statesman*, October 21, 1911.
[196] National Council, "Vital Statistics," 37.
[197] "KGC," CNY Artifact Recovery.
[198] Williams, "1891, the Year of the African American Postmistress."
[199] American Missionary Association, "Our Spring Associations."
[200] North Carolina, Marriage Index, 1741–2004, "H.R. Walden and Eleanor W. Walden."

[201] Hampton Institute, "Henry Walden," 290.

[202] Lewis, "North Carolina Education."

[203] American Missionary Association, "Obituary: Mrs. Henry R. Walden."

[204] North Carolina, Marriage Index, 1741–2004, "H.R. Walden and Theodosia Hargrove."

[205] North Carolina, Marriage Records, 1741–2011, "Catherine Hill and Shubal Ingram."

[206] To learn more about the educational achievements of Strieby School, see Williams, *From Hill Town to Strieby*.

[207] Williams, *From Hill Town to Strieby*.

[208] Ibid.

[209] Randolph County, North Carolina Historic Landmark and Preservation Commission [hereafter HLPC], "Meeting Minutes, September 23, 2014"; HLPC, "Strieby Church Cultural Heritage Site"; Penkava, "Strieby Church Named Cultural Heritage Site"; Walker, "Strieby Church, School, and Cemetery"; Williams, *History of Strieby Congregational Church*; Williams, "Once upon a Time."

Appendix: Ancestry of Islay Walden

[210] This section is based on the author's blog post "Will Anderson Walden Please Stand?"

[211] North Carolina, Wills and Probate Records, 1665–1998, "William Walden, Probate Date"

[212] 1840 USFC.

[213] 1850 USFC.

[214] 1860 USFC.

[215] 1870 USFC.

[216] North Carolina, Marriage Records, 1741–2011, "Haywood Walden and Lucrettie Walden."

[217] 1870 USFC.

[218] USFC Mortality Schedules, 1850–1885, "Anderson Walden."

[219] North Carolina, Marriage Records, 1741–2011, "Anderson Walden and Sally Walden."

[220] 1850 USFC.

[221] 1860 USFC.

[222] 1870 USFC.

[223] USFC Mortality Schedules, 1850–1885, "Anderson Walden."

[224] 1870 USFC.

[225] Ibid.

[226] Ibid.

[227] H.R. Walden, "John Walden," in *Family Record of Anderson and Julia Walden*, 8.

[228] 1870 USFC.

[229] 1900 USFC.

[230] North Carolina, Marriage Records, 1741–2011, "Alfred I. Walden and Amelia Frances Harriss."

[231] *Evening Post*, "Interesting Ordination."

[232] Williams, *From Hill Town to Strieby*, 93–98.

[233] North Carolina, Marriage Index, 1741–2004, "H.R. Walden and Eleanor W. Walden."

[234] Find a Grave, "Strieby Congregational United Church of Christ Cemetery."

[235] Find a Grave, "Strieby United Church of Christ Cemetery."

[236] 1850 USFC.

[237] 1870 USFC.

[238] Ibid.

[239] Ibid.

[240] 1850 USFC.

[241] Ibid.

[242] Ibid.

[243] 1840 USFC.

[244] 1879 USFC.

[245] North Carolina, Marriage Records, 1741–2011, "Anderson Walden and Sally Walden."

[246] 1850 USFC.

[247] U.S. Federal Census Mortality Schedules, 1850–1885, "Anderson Walden."

[248] Ibid.

[249] H.R. Walden, "Julia and Anderson Walden," in *Family Record of Anderson and Julia Walden*, 4–5.

[250] Ibid.

[251] Ibid., 4; Find a Grave, "Strieby Congregational United Church of Christ Cemetery."

[252] H.R. Walden, "Her Christian Character," in *Family Record of Anderson and Julia Walden*, 8–10.

Made in the USA
Monee, IL
24 May 2022

96926480R10085